# Guideposts
# The Joys of Christmas 2011

"I truly *believe* that if we keep telling the Christmas story, singing the Christmas songs and living the Christmas *spirit*, *we can bring joy and happiness and peace to this world.*"

—Norman Vincent Peale

GUIDEPOSTS, *a nonprofit organization, touches millions of lives every day through products and services that inspire, encourage and uplift. Our magazines, books, prayer network and outreach programs help people connect their faith-filled values to their daily lives. To learn more, visit* **guideposts.org/about** *or* **guidepostsfoundation.org**.

# Table *of* Contents



* ENJOY THESE GUIDEPOSTS CLASSICS!

TOP: JOHN VON DORN; BOTTOM LEFT: PAUL PUGLIESE; BOTTOM RIGHT: ROSS MACDONALD

72

78




*Guideposts* The Joys of Christmas *is published annually by Guideposts, 39 Old Ridgebury Road, Suite 2AB, Danbury, CT 06810. Canadian GST #893989236.*



*Volume 03, No. 1. Printed in U.S.A. Send address changes to Guideposts, P.O. Box 5815, Harlan, IA 51593-1315.*

TOP: KATE BALDWIN; BOTTOM: REBECCA SAHN

# Bethlehem

A little child,
A shining star.
A stable rude,
The door ajar.
Yet in that place,
So crude, forlorn,
The Hope of all
The world was born.
*—Anonymous*

# The Christmas Star

May the Light that shone
From the Christmas Star
On that night so long ago
Fall on you this Christmas night
And set your face aglow.
May it shine from your eyes.
May it rest in your mind.
May it burn in your Spirit bright.
May the Peace it spoke to a weary world
Bring joy to your heart tonight.
*—Mary Garren*

# A Letter from the Editor

HEY, THIS is getting to be a tradition, right? This is our third—and we think best—GUIDEPOSTS *The Joys of Christmas*, and if you are a new reader let me (and Millie) be the first to wish you glad tidings. If you've been with us longer, thank you for making us a part of your holiday season.

Christmas is the time we spend with people we love. Most of all, family. Very early I learned this was one of the great blessings of the season. I was named by my sister after her favorite uncle. I was supposed to be John—my mom loved that name—but Mary Lou was so upset when Mom went into the hospital to have me that my parents relented and promised Mary Lou she could pick the name. She adored Uncle Eddie, my father's fun-loving, pipe-smoking younger brother. So Edward I was, born exactly two weeks before Christmas.

I grew to love Uncle Eddie too. He wore funky hats, drove sports cars and was always up for adventure. He lived in Indianapolis with his wife, Agnes, and was a research biochemist. He and Aunt Agnes would spend Christmas with us outside Detroit and I was always even more excited about Eddie's arrival than about Santa's. One Christmas Eve the weather slowed them down and I was ushered to bed before they got there. "Go to sleep," Mom said. "We'll open presents after church in the morning." Sleep? Not a chance. I lay awake waiting for the sweep of headlights through the window, the telltale crunch of tires in the driveway. Santa? I had my doubts about him. But I knew Uncle Eddie would come. Then I heard it, the sound of a car. I crept to my window and peered out. The snow had stopped and stars were poking through the sky. It was Eddie and Agnes and a little bundle that held my cousin Gloria. My parents were bringing them inside, everyone carrying suitcases and presents.

For a long time I stared at their footprints in the fresh snow beneath my window, the footprints of my family. It filled me with such gladness and awe that even now, all these years later, that little ember of a Christmas memory still glows.

I hope something glows for you this year...a moment or a memory or simply the company of the people you love. Because that is what Christmas is, the time when we can count our blessings like footprints in the snow.

**EDWARD GRINNAN, Editor-in-Chief, GUIDEPOSTS**

JANE WEXLER

# 2011 Advent

| SUNDAY | MONDAY | TUESDAY |
|---|---|---|
| FIRST SUNDAY<br>**November 27**<br>Prepare your hearts. *"Behold, the virgin shall conceive and bear a son, and they shall call his name Emmanuel (which means, God with us)."* (Matthew 1:23) | **28**<br>Download your favorite Christmas music onto your iPod. | **29**<br>Dear God, help me to get caught up not in the business but in the blessings. |
| SECOND SUNDAY<br>**December 4**<br>Celebrate the good news. *"And the angel said to them, 'Fear not, for behold, I bring you good news of great joy that will be for all the people.'"* (Luke 2:10) | **5**<br>Share a childhood Christmas memory with the children in your family. | **6**<br>Write a thank-you to your letter carrier for delivering all those cards! |
| THIRD SUNDAY<br>**December 11**<br>Look for signs of God's love. *"And this will be a sign for you: you will find a baby wrapped in swaddling cloths and lying in a manger."* (Luke 2:12) | **12**<br>Write simple activity cards for kids. Have them pick one—making paper snowflakes, baking cookies—each day. | **13**<br>Traveling? Recall the journey of the Three Wise Men. |
| FOURTH SUNDAY<br>**December 18**<br>Praise God. *"Glory to God in the highest, and on earth peace among those with whom he is pleased!"* (Luke 2:13, 14) | **19**<br>A gift for pet lovers: Donate a bag of pet food to a shelter in their honor. | **20**<br>Collect Christmas cards you receive with Nativity scenes. Marvel at the different ways the scene is depicted. |

IT'S CHRISTMAS!

**December 25**

Rejoice! *"For unto you is born this day in the city of David a Savior, who is Christ the Lord."* (Luke 2:11)

**Joy to the World!**

# Calendar

| WEDNESDAY | THURSDAY | FRIDAY | SATURDAY |
|---|---|---|---|
| **30** Send Christmas cards that benefit a cause, such as the ASPCA or the American Diabetes Association. | **December 1** Kids, add one construction paper link to a paper chain every day till Christmas. Say a prayer with each. | **2** Make the crèche the focal point of your decorations. Give it a place of honor and visit often. | **3** Bake extra treats for people who serve at the hospital or police or fire stations. |
| **7** Recite the names of Jesus: Wonderful Counselor, Mighty God, Everlasting Father, Prince of Peace… | **8** Stumped for a gift? Write a book of prayers, tailor-made for a special person. | **9** Join your church or community for caroling. Or sing by yourself, at the top of your lungs! | **10** Host a Christmas cookie party. Everyone brings their favorite kind and takes home a plate of each. |
| **14** Decorate a backyard tree with popcorn and cranberries for the birds. | **15** Recycle Christmas cards. Cut a shape from the picture on front. Write "TO:" and "FROM:" on back. Instant gift tag! | **16** Take a ride to see the lights. Say a prayer for the residents of each home as you admire the decorations. | **17** Break out the sleeping bags. Let the kids camp out under the tree. |
| **21** Make easy ornaments: ¾ cup applesauce and 4 ounces cinnamon. Roll, cut with cookie cutters. Air dry. | **22** Find the brightest star in the sky. Imagine the brightness of the Star of Bethlehem! | **23** Wear matching pajamas. Don't forget to take a picture! | **24** Dim the lights, gather together under the tree and read the story of Christ's birth. |

ILLUSTRATION BY ROBIN MOLINE

PETER LAMASTRO

# The Joy of Traditions

*"Along with Christmas belong the keepsakes and the customs."*

*—Marjorie Holmes*

# The Bluebird Stocking

## A new family tradition—good deeds done in the name of love

**by Sharon Mangas, Columbus, Indiana**

THE JUNIOR League Holiday Mart was in full swing. My best friend, Mary Ann, and I wandered through the rows of vendor booths, the smell of gourmet chocolates and fresh-baked cookies wafting through the air. Carols piped over the speakers. It was enough to get anyone into the Christmas spirit. Anyone but me. I couldn't stop thinking about Mom. Ever since she'd died, five years earlier, Christmas hadn't felt the same.

Mom loved everything about Christmas. She would've enjoyed the Holiday Mart—all the proceeds went toward bettering the community. When I was growing up Mom donated books and toys, hand-delivering them to needy children during the holidays. That wasn't easy for a widow raising three little girls on her own.

"Check out these handmade stockings," Mary Ann said. Making my way over I passed a mom and daughter shopping for ornaments. My sisters and I loved finding the right gift for Mom at Christmas. A pair of slippers, a great book or, best of all, a bluebird, Mom's favorite. "Bluebirds stand for happiness," she'd say, and launch into "Somewhere Over the Rainbow," while arranging her cherished collection of ceramic, porcelain and wooden bluebirds from all over the world.

"Each stocking's prettier than the next," Mary Ann said. She was right. I picked up one in rich green velvet with gold trim. And that's when I saw it: a delicate needlepoint stocking with a bluebird on it.

"I think you should buy it," Mary Ann said. "In honor of your mom."

She couldn't be serious. "Hanging an empty stocking for Mom would just make me miss her even more."

"Who says it has to be empty? Your mom did so much for others. Why don't you ask everyone in your family to do a good deed in her memory, write it down and send it to you. Tuck each note in the bluebird stocking, then read the deeds aloud on Christmas morning. E-mail them to anyone who can't be there."

What a good idea! Just buying the stocking would help the community in a small way, but starting a new tradition of helping others? That was even better.

ILLUSTRATION BY TOM NEWSOM

"Well...?" Mary Ann said. "Is it a plan?"

I wrapped her in a hug. "What are we waiting for?"

Christmas morning the bluebird stocking hung over the fireplace. The family gathered round as I pulled out the notes inside: a goat for a needy family in Haiti, presents for a single mom and her children, a generous tip for a struggling waitress, a box of brand-new books for a public school.

Empty stocking? No way. It's overflowing with love and generosity in memory of Mom. And me? I'm filled with the Christmas spirit, again!

# Something Missing

## I liked my Nativities arranged with *all* the pieces, thank you very much

**by Marguerite Gray, Ferriday, Louisiana**

ADVENT HAD just begun, and I couldn't wait to set out my Nativity sets. I had 11 in all. My 15-year-old daughter, Katie, and I went around the house, setting them up in different places. Ceramic figures on the mantel, Jerusalem olive wood on the bookcase, silver-plated on a side table. Christmas comes but once a year, so why not celebrate it all month long?

A couple of weeks later I got another reason to celebrate. "Your mother and I thought we'd drop by next Sunday," my dad told me over the phone one afternoon. Mama didn't travel much during the Christmas season. She had too many people coming to see her and too much going on at her church. We'd never missed a Christmas visit to Mama's house, but I couldn't remember the last time she'd visited me in December. *She hasn't seen half the Nativities in my collection,* I thought as I hung up. Even the Baby Jesus lying in his manger on the shelf by the phone seemed excited.

Mama and Daddy's visit was on the second Sunday of Advent. "Welcome!" I said, waving my hand with a flourish across the living room. I beamed as Mama took in all my decorations. The angels and Santas, the greenery.

Mama's eyes fell on something just over my shoulder. Whatever it was she didn't like what she saw. I turned and followed her gaze to a hand-painted Nativity. "What's wrong?" I asked.

"What on earth is Jesus doing there in Advent?" Mama demanded. "We leave the manger empty until Christmas Day."

I started to tell Mama how I enjoyed the sight of the Christ Child in the manger far too much to wait for Christmas Day like we'd done growing up. "Why not celebrate all month?" I said.

Mama was having none of it.

"This simply won't do," she said. "I thought I taught you better than this." She plucked the Baby Jesus from his manger. Then she went to the Nativity from Ecuador on an end table and took that Baby Jesus too.

"What is she doing?" I whispered to Daddy.

"I have no idea," he said.

Mama ran to the bookcase and grabbed

PHOTOS BY TIM MUELLER

**REUNITED** *Marguerite with her collection of Nativity sets*

the Baby Jesus from the Nativity made of olive wood. Then she went into the den. The rest of us followed far behind. Somehow it seemed wise to keep our distance.

When Mama was finished every manger was empty—and so were her hands. When she came back there was not a Baby Jesus in sight. "Where have you put them?" I said.

"You'll find out on Christmas morning," she said. "The day when Jesus was born."

I didn't want to argue. Mama was set in her ways. Besides, it was only a figurine, and I had plenty of other decorations. But I couldn't let her leave the house without knowing where they were. "Where did you hide the baby Jesuses?" I asked as she and Daddy got ready to leave.

"You'll know when it's time, sweetheart," she said, giving me a kiss and Katie a big hug.

The next morning when I got up the first thing I noticed was Jesus' empty manger on the bookcase. And the mantel. And the end table. Empty, empty, empty. *Where could she have put them?* I wondered. I looked under the sofa and behind the big dresser. I checked the mangers again, half hoping that the Baby Jesus had magically reappeared while I searched. *You'll just have to wait,* I told myself. Two weeks wasn't so long, was it?

A few days later I got up early, made a cup of hot tea and sat down next to the tree in the living room with my Bible. I was barely able to read a line before my eyes

**AWAY IN A MANGER**
*Marguerite now waits until Christmas Day to bring out the baby Jesuses.*

drifted to the hand-painted Nativity on the dresser. I looked in the empty cradle and imagined the baby finally lying there. *How many days now?*

Jesus had always just been there for me. Like a figurine I pulled out of a box. I'd never imagined what the world was like before Jesus, what it would be like to be told of his coming and then having to wait... and wait. Christmas was still 10 days away. I looked at the faces of Mary and Joseph, gazing down at the manger in—what was it?—anticipation, hopefulness, longing? The only emotion I could muster was impatience. What if Mama forgot where she'd put the baby Jesuses? What if this year the Christ Child wasn't coming? "I don't know how you managed to wait that long for him," I told the hand-painted Mary. "I'm not waiting another minute."

I GOT UP FROM the couch and combed the house. Again. I searched the pantry, rummaged through the hall closet, reached way behind the TV. It was no use. I couldn't find them. There was nothing to do but hope... and pray.

Usually in December when I would read the prophecies in the Bible my mind raced ahead to Jesus' birth. But this year I read through those prophecies carefully, marveling at the faith and fortitude God had asked of his people. I wondered if I would still have believed after all those years. I had even started to doubt that I'd see my Jesus figurines again. *This is what it feels like to wait,* I thought, staring again at the empty mangers.

Each morning after that my anticipation grew, the familiar story suddenly like a novel I couldn't put down. I felt Mary's fear at the angel's pronouncement. The questions she must have had. Then the worry and distress of finding no room at the inn. After everything they'd gone through. For the first time I really understood what it meant to walk in faith, trusting that God—and Mama—would be true to their word. I hadn't thought of waiting as being a part of Christmas since I was a little girl. Jesus was coming! It wouldn't be long now.

On Christmas Eve the phone rang. It was Daddy. He asked for Katie. "Uh-huh," she said, a smile creeping across her face as she listened. She turned to me when she hung up. "You'll never believe where they are," she said. Then she walked out of the room without telling me!

That night I barely slept a wink. I got up while it was still dark. It was here. December 25. Christmas Day! Was Katie ever going to wake up?

Finally my sleepyhead daughter shuffled out of her room. "Ready?" she said. She led us all into the living room. I sat on the couch. Katie went to the dresser, not two feet away from where I'd read my Bible. *How could I have missed them there?* I thought. Katie pulled open a drawer and cupped the Baby Jesuses in her hand, lifting them into the air. *Hallelujah!* rang in my head.

We went from room to room delivering each Christ Child to a waiting Mary and Joseph. I knew how the angels must have felt that glorious night heralding Jesus' birth. I was bursting with excitement. Like no Christmas I'd ever experienced before.

Mama called just after breakfast. "Merry Christmas," I told her. "And thanks for the gift. It's one I'll never forget."

Every year now when I set out my Nativities I put all the baby Jesuses in the dresser by the front door. It's my most cherished family tradition. Christmas is coming. And it is well worth the wait.

Watch our video of a Christmas tradition at the Metropolitan Museum of Art in New York City. Go to **guideposts.org/angeltree**

# Ring in the Cheer!

## Making music with my teenager

**by Lisa Bogart, San Rafael, California**

CHRISTMAS EVE I stood in the back of the church, waiting for the moment our handbell choir would open the service. My son, Zach, and I, in the treble section, playing two-in-hand, would ring our way through "O Little Town of Bethlehem" and "Silent Night" and "It Came Upon a Midnight Clear," the joyful sound echoing down the aisle. But my joy was tempered. One of the other members had reminded me: "Zach will be away at college next year, won't he?"

It had been just five years since the handbell choir started up and I asked Zach, then a lanky eighth grader, if he wanted to give it a try. "Sure," he said. Other teens joined us at first, but Zach was the only one who stuck it out. How I would miss those Monday night rehearsals, standing next to him, learning our parts together. I'd played handbells all through high school and college, but Zach caught up to me quickly. He was good at it, whispering a tricky rhythm in my ear, mastering the challenge of holding four bells at once.

One night when I was struggling through a tough arrangement of Tchaikovsky's "Russian Dance" from *The Nutcracker Suite,* I asked him, "Want to switch parts?" Twice through and he was ringing two-in-hand without missing a beat. Zach played clarinet in the school band, but this was our chance to make music together. Soon he would be gone.

We walked to the front of the church and took up our positions. I looked out at the congregation and saw young children sitting in their parents' laps. It didn't seem so long ago that Zach had sat that way in mine. Now he towered over me. Next year I'd be up here on my own, and he'd be in the congregation like the other kids home from college. He was ready to move on—more than I was. I had to let him go.

We picked up the bells and started playing. All at once I found the comfort I was looking for. It was in the music, this tradition we'd shared all those Monday nights. I realized how lucky I'd been to pass on what I loved, this music that set my faith soaring. He'd have it no matter where he went, ringing in his ears, the tunes echoing in his heart, like the peal of the bells filling the church with the sound of Christmas year after year.

**CHIMING IN** *Lisa and Zach play "two-in-hand."*

NICKIE FRYE

# Scrooge *Revisited*

## Discover how a young woman finds a new and personal meaning in Dickens's beloved classic *A Christmas Carol*

**by Rosie Schaap, Brooklyn, New York**

B*AH, HUMBUG!?* That was never really my style. I *loved* Christmas when I was growing up. I couldn't wait until my mother put up our tree and let my brother and me carefully hang up the ornaments she'd collected over the years. Even my annual holiday chore—the onerous task of detangling the strings of lights—didn't faze me: I'd sit on the floor and patiently tease them out of the great big knot they'd become in storage, while listening to my parents' old LPs of Bing Crosby and Ella Fitzgerald singing all of my holiday favorites. Then, come Christmas morning, I was always the first in the family to bolt out of bed at the crack of dawn to open the beautifully wrapped and beribboned gifts that waited under the tree. Home never felt more like home—imbued with warmth and good cheer, full of music and laughter and love—than it did at Christmastime.

But lately Christmas has lost much of its joy for me. My husband, Frank, died early last year—at age 42—after a courageous fight against a rare form of cancer. That would be reason enough to feel down around the holidays. But what makes it even harder is that Frank's birthday was December 24, Christmas Eve. You can see why I don't feel as festive as I once did.

Frank was a scholar of British literature. In some ways he seemed like the perfect example of the absent-minded professor: deeply intelligent, funny and kind, devoted to his students, often harried and a bit scattered (which I always attributed to the fact that he held so much information in his mind—it must have been impossible to keep his many ideas and thoughts perfectly ordered). He left a trail of papers and books and notes jotted on napkins wherever he went, but always managed to find whatever text or passage he needed. Frank's work focused primarily on the English Romantic poets—especially Wordsworth and Keats. But he read widely and voraciously, with speed I always envied, and one of his other great literary loves was Charles Dickens.

Like my late husband, I love Dickens, but I have to admit that his most popular book, *A Christmas Carol,* kind of left me cold. Compared with my favorites—especially *Bleak House* and *Great Expectations,* long, complex novels from Dickens's late period—*A Christmas Carol* seemed skimpy and a little trite.

But recently I pulled it off the bookshelf and reread it for the first time since I was a child, and I realized I'd completely misjudged it. The critic Roger Rosenblatt called *A Christmas Carol* "the best story ever written." He may be right. It's a fantastic story. And a profound one too.

Its main character, Ebenezer Scrooge, is pretty hard to love, at least when the reader first meets him: a bitter and stingy man in his countinghouse on Christmas Eve, rebuking anyone who dares wish him a Merry Christmas with that infamous exclamation *"Bah, humbug!"* He treats his clerk, the hardworking and kindhearted Bob Cratchit, with scorn and meanness, grudgingly conceding that he is permitted to take Christmas Day off, but insisting that he return to work especially early on the following day. When men collecting for charity come to his door, he refuses to part with any of his considerable wealth to help the poor people of London (and there were many impoverished Londoners in Dickens's day). Scrooge even contemptuously declines his well-meaning nephew Fred's invitation to Christmas dinner.

But you remember what happens next, right? On Christmas Eve, Scrooge encounters the ghost of his former business partner, Jacob Marley, who warns him that he will be visited by three more ghosts: one of Christmas Past, the next of Christmas Present and the third of Christmas Yet-to-Come. The Spirit of Christmas Past guides Scrooge—and the reader—through his harsh and lonely childhood, his disappointments and sufferings, which helps us understand why he behaves the way he does. The Spirit of Christmas Present brings Scrooge to the humble home of the Cratchit family, who, despite their relative poverty, clearly love each other and celebrate the holiday joyfully. Not least joyful is the youngest of the children, Tiny Tim, who uses crutches and, tragically, is expected to die soon. And finally, when the

**SECOND READ** *Always a Dickens fan, Rosie didn't appreciate his famous ghost story until tragedy struck her life.*

REBECCA SAHN

**"GOD BLESS US, EVERY ONE"**
*Charles Dickens made sure Bob Cratchit and his son Tiny Tim didn't let poverty spoil the joy of Christmas.*

Grim Reaper-like Ghost of Christmas Yet-to-Come presents Scrooge with a vision of his possible future—the future that will come to pass if he does not change his ways and treat people with kindness, generosity and Christmas cheer—Scrooge is shaken to his core. The thought of dying unloved and unremembered is unbearable to him.

Presented with the precious opportunity to change course, Scrooge seizes it. Who wouldn't? He undergoes a complete turnaround by the end of the book: Overtaken by Christmas spirit, he sends the Cratchit family the best and biggest turkey he can buy, gives Bob a raise and makes it to his nephew Fred's home in time for the party.

Charles Dickens wrote most of his books in serial form; Victorian readers followed his novels the way we follow favorite television series now, and they couldn't wait for the latest installment to be printed so they could find out what happened next. *A Christmas Carol* is an exception. It's a short book, published in a single volume, which Dickens wrote very quickly over the course of about six weeks in 1843, when he was in debt and badly needed to earn money. Although Dickens was known to be generous, the character of Ebenezer Scrooge represents one aspect of the writer himself: a man frequently preoccupied by finances. (There are other parallels: Like Scrooge, the author had a sister called Fanny.)

DICKENS was the son of neglectful and irresponsible parents, who declined from relatively comfortable middle-class life to utter pennilessness in the course of Dickens's boyhood. It is hard to imagine that Charles's Christmases were joyful occasions. According to Norrie Epstein, author of *The Friendly Dickens,* "the worst day of his childhood was December 25, 1822, the day he traveled from Chatham to London, leaving behind the happiest days of his life." At 12 Charles was sent to work at Warren's Blacking Warehouse; at the same time, his father was confined in a debtors' prison. Dickens grew up knowing hardship, hunger and want. And when he started to find success in his career as a writer, he strove for financial stability, and continued to fret about money for much of his life. A constant concern in his writing is that children need and deserve proper childhoods—instead of being treated as miniature adults. Writing many years later of his dismal, rat-infested place of youthful employment, Dickens conveys the trauma of the experience: "I never had the courage to go back to the place where my servitude began," he said. "I could not endure to go near it."

It's not surprising that this little book, written out of a sense of economic urgency, not only took hold of its many readers, but also of its author, who deeply yearned for Christmas cheer. Dickens gave numerous public readings of the book (he'd once hoped to be an actor, and dramatically performed the story in multiple voices), sometimes to raise money for the kinds of charities resisted so strongly by Scrooge. And he was said to be as moved as his audience—perhaps even more deeply—by the plight of Tiny Tim, who, we learn with immense relief at the book's conclusion, "did NOT die."

Peter Ackroyd observes, in his biography of Dickens, that the great author "had an acute sense of, and need for, 'Home'—it sprang from his own experience of being banished from that blessed place—which is why in *A Christmas Carol*...there is a constant contrast between warmth and cold, between the domestic interior and the noisome streets, between the rich and the poor...between the need for comfort and the anxiety about homelessness." Ackroyd's thoughtful analysis helped me to understand why my latest reading of Dickens's beloved story hit me harder than it ever had before. Since Frank died, "home" is not what it once was.

And it never will be the same. I accept that. Few among us go through our lives without enduring losses that feel impossible to bear, without losing people we love and missing them forever. I miss Frank every day, and most of all during the season of his birth, the season of Christmas. On Frank's birthday, of course I will be thinking of him. I learned a lot from my husband about literature, but his most enduring lesson, taught by example, was about how to live: *Be kind.* And, in the end, isn't that Dickens's message in *A Christmas Carol*? So I don't feel cynical or sad when I read Tiny Tim Cratchit's celebrated benediction with which *A Christmas Carol* concludes: "God Bless Us, Every One." No matter how deeply I feel this loss, I *do* feel blessed—for having known Frank, for the time we spent together. And whenever I pick a volume of Dickens off the bookshelves we once shared and open it up to read, I feel as though we are still connected, and that Frank is with me, reading over my shoulder.

**REBORN**
*Ebenezer Scrooge is a truly changed man after his ghostly visitations on Christmas Eve.*

# Make a Wreath, *Make a Christmas*

## Past, present and future, all woven together

by Jeanne Tromp, Rhinelander, Wisconsin

FLORIDA isn't like Wisconsin. The woods full of princess pine where Mom and I used to gather boughs for our Christmas wreaths don't exist in this climate. But my daughters wanted to make wreaths anyway.

"It's a Thanksgiving tradition," Jen insisted.

"You can take one home with you to Wisconsin for Christmas," Jessica told me.

**WITH PINECONES AND BERRIES** *Jeanne and her daughters, Jessica and Jennifer, gather branches in Jeanne's backyard.*

PHOTOS BY JOHN VON DORN

Wreaths weren't just something to hang on the door in my family. They were woven into Christmas itself. But I found I wasn't looking forward to making them this year. This was the first holiday season since Mom had died, and my heart wasn't in it. I had come to visit the girls in Florida to take my mind off Christmas and the happy memories of Mom that were all wrapped up with it. Had I lost my Christmas spirit forever?

"There aren't any woods here," I said, hoping the girls would forget the idea.

"There are plenty of craft stores, though," Jessica said. "It'll be fun!"

They dragged me to a shopping center. Walking through aisles of craft supplies wasn't the same as walking through the woods with Mom. As I ran my hand over the displays of ribbons, bows, feathers and sequins, I remembered the crispness of the chilly air in the fall, the brilliant colors of the leaves. Sometimes Mom and I would even catch sight of a deer bounding off in the distance, or a partridge hiding among the tree roots. *It's just not Christmas without her,* I thought. When Mom twisted those branches onto a metal frame it was

as if she were making Christmas joyous. With her own hands. How could I ever re-create that?

Jen and Jessica appeared with a shopping cart full of artificial tree branches and pinecones—plus a pile of feathers and beads. "We'll make the best wreaths yet," they said.

When we got home Jen spread the supplies out on the kitchen table. Jessica popped in a Bing Crosby Christmas CD. They were so excited about the wreaths I didn't have the heart not to join in.

"Mom, what am I doing wrong?" Jen asked, holding up a half-made wreath. "My branches aren't lying flat the way yours are."

"It's easy," I said. "Let me show you how I do it."

The girls watched carefully as I wove the branch in and out of the wreath frame just the way Mom had taught me. I'd watched her do it dozens of times. *Now Jennifer and Jessica will learn from me,* I thought. Maybe they'd learn to weave happy memories into sad times and make something beautiful in a new way.

I plucked a feather from the pile and added it to the wreath I was working on. I heard someone humming along with Bing Crosby and realized it was me. I looked down at the wreath. *I'm doing it,* I thought. *I'm making Christmas joy. Just like Mom.*

By the end of the day we'd finished two wreaths, one for Jen and one for Jessica. They didn't look exactly like the wreaths I'd made with Mom all those years. But somehow that didn't matter. They were still beautiful. Our family wreath-making was evolving as our lives changed. Past, present and future, all woven together and made new each year by our own hands and in our own hearts, where Christmas spirit can always be found.

# How to Make

**STEP 1** *You'll need a 12-inch wreath ring, florist's wire, pinecones, 3 feet of ribbon, wire cutters, real or artificial pine branches, plastic berries, other ornaments.*

**STEP 4** *Wrap wire around pinecones and berries and attach to wreath ring. Take 6 to 8 inches of wire and fold in half. Attach one end to wreath, make a hook out of the other.*

# a Wreath It's easy to start your own tradition!

**STEP 2** *Separate the greens into small bunches; tie each bunch together with wire.*

**STEP 3** *Starting at the bottom, weave the end of each bunch into the ring wires; fasten with florist's wire.*

**STEP 5** *Tie ribbon into a bow and attach to wreath ring with wire. Hang and enjoy.*

# Our Christmas Angels

**The role of angels in the Christmas story has ignited the imagination of artists for centuries. Behold these beautiful renderings of God's blessed messengers!**

## The angel Gabriel appears to Mary

The angel Gabriel was sent from God to a town of Galilee named Nazareth to a virgin betrothed to a man whose name was Joseph. The virgin's name was Mary. And he came to her and said, "Hail, O favored one, the Lord is with you!" But she was greatly troubled at the saying, and considered what sort of greeting this might be.

And the angel said to her, "Do not be afraid, Mary, for you have found favor with God. Behold, you will conceive and bear a son, and you shall call his name Jesus. He will be great, and will be called the Son of the Most High; and the Lord God will give to him the throne of his father David, and he will reign over the house of Jacob forever; and of his kingdom there will be no end."

Mary replied, "How shall this be, since I have no husband?"

The angel said to her, "The Holy Spirit will come upon you, and the power of the Most High will overshadow you; therefore, the child to be born will be called holy, the Son of God. And behold, your cousin Elizabeth in her old age has also conceived a son. For with God nothing will be impossible."

Mary said, "Behold, I am the handmaid of the Lord. Let it be to me according to your word." And the angel departed from her. Mary arose and went with haste to a city in Judah, and she entered the house of Zechariah and greeted Elizabeth. When Elizabeth heard the greeting, the babe leaped in her womb and Elizabeth was filled with the Holy Spirit. She exclaimed with a loud cry, "Blessed are you among women, and blessed is the fruit of your womb!" —Luke 1:26–43

*This page: oil on canvas, c. 1638 (detail), artist unknown; opposite: oil on copper plate, by Carl Heinrich Bloch (1834–90)*

ANTOINE AND LOUIS LE NAIN/GETTY IMAGES

*Fresco, paint on plaster, in the Arena Chapel, Padua, Italy, by Giotto di Bondone (1266/70–1337)*



## An angel appears to Joseph

Now the birth of Jesus took place in this way. When Mary had been betrothed to Joseph, before they came together she was found to be with child of the Holy Spirit, and her husband, Joseph, being a just man and unwilling to put her to shame, resolved to divorce her quietly.

But as he considered this, behold, an angel of the Lord appeared to him in a dream, saying, "Joseph, son of David, do not fear to take Mary for your wife, for that which is conceived in her is of the Holy Spirit. She will bear a son, and you shall call his name Jesus, for he will save his people from their sins." All this took place to fulfill what the Lord had spoken by the prophet: "Behold, a virgin shall conceive and bear a son, and his name shall be called Emmanuel," which means, God with us.

When Joseph woke from sleep, he did as the angel of the Lord commanded him. He took his wife but knew her not until she had borne a son, and he called his name Jesus. —Matthew 1:18–25

## The angels come to the shepherds

In those days a decree went out from Caesar Augustus that all the world should be enrolled. This was the first enrollment, and it was made when Quirinius was governor of Syria. And all went to be enrolled, each to his own city. Joseph went up from Galilee, from the city of Nazareth, to Judea, to the city of David, which is called Bethlehem, because he was of the house and lineage of David, to be enrolled with Mary, his betrothed who was with child. While they were there, the time came for her to be delivered. And she gave birth to her first-born son and wrapped him in swaddling cloths and laid him in a manger because there was no place for them in the inn.

In that region there were shepherds out in the field, keeping watch over their flock by night. An angel of the Lord appeared to them and the glory of the Lord shone around them and they were filled with fear.

The angel said to them, "Be not afraid. For behold, I bring you good news of a great joy which will come to all people. To you is born this day in the city of David a Savior, who is Christ the Lord. This will be a sign for you. You will find a babe wrapped in swaddling cloths lying in a manger."

Suddenly there was with the angel a multitude of the heavenly host praising God and saying, "Glory to God in the highest and peace to his people on earth."

When the angels went away from them into heaven, the shepherds said to one another, "Let us now go over to Bethlehem and see this thing that has happened, which the Lord has made known to us."

And they went with haste and found both Mary and Joseph, and the babe lying in a manger. When they saw it they made known the saying which had been told them concerning this child, and all who heard it wondered at what the shepherds told them.

But Mary kept all these things, pondering them in her heart. And the shepherds returned, glorifying and praising God for all they had heard and seen as it had been told them. —Luke 2:1–20

GETTY IMAGES

*Nostalgia card (left), by Clara M. Burd (1873–1933); oil on canvas (right), by Julius Schnorr von Carolsfeld (1794–1872)*



## An angel alerts Joseph in a dream

Now when Jesus was born in Bethlehem in the days of Herod the king, wise men from the East came to Jerusalem, saying, "Where is he who was born king of the Jews? For we have seen his star in the East and have come to worship him."

When Herod the king heard this he was troubled and all Jerusalem with him, and assembling all the chief priests and scribes of the people, he inquired of them where the Christ was to be born. They told him, "In Bethlehem of Judea, for so it is written by the prophet."

Then Herod summoned the wise men secretly and ascertained from them what time the star appeared and he sent them to Bethlehem, saying, "Go and search diligently for the child, and when you have found him bring me word, that I too may come and worship him."

When they had heard the king they went their way and lo, the star which they had seen in the East went before them till it came to rest over the place where the child was. When they saw the star, they rejoiced exceedingly with great joy, and going into the house they saw the child with Mary his mother and they fell down and worshipped him. Then, opening their treasures, they offered him gifts, gold and frankincense and myrrh. And being warned in a dream not to return to Herod, they departed to their own country by another way.

Now when they had departed, an angel of the Lord appeared to Joseph in a dream and said, "Rise, take the child and his mother and flee to Egypt and remain there till I tell you, for Herod is about to search for the child to destroy him." And he rose and took the child and his mother to Egypt, and remained there until the death of Herod.

—Matthew 2:1-15

# Mysterious

## *Mother's* Last Words

Guideposts Classic 1983

WE LIVED on a farm in the mountains of Virginia, and for many years my mother made her home with us. But one morning Mother woke up completely disoriented, and during the years that followed, she grew progressively worse. Her ability to communicate with anyone was gone. I felt numb about her silent condition, as though she were lost to us and, it seemed to me, lost to God as well.

Just before Christmas some carolers came over the hills. The group of young people—led by Miss Winnie and Miss Naomi, two missionaries from our church, and our pastor's wife, Phyllis—sang in the snow outside our door. Then I hustled everyone into our big, warm kitchen for hot chocolate and cookies. I took the three ladies into Mother's room, and Phyllis leaned over the bed and said, "Grandmother, it's Christmas."

No response.

Phyllis took her hand and said again, "Grandmother, do you know what Christmas is?"

Then it happened. Mother's eyes flew open, and it was as if a light had been turned on behind them; an angelic smile spread over her worn features, and in a strong, normal voice she replied, "Oh, yes! It is the birthday of my precious Savior."

Now we eagerly plied Mother with questions, but it was over. Those were the last words that Mother ever spoke, but they were enough. I knew beyond a shadow of a doubt that the birth of Jesus Christ has a power beyond anything we can consciously comprehend. And that Mother was in his hands forever.

*Betty Banner*
*Jackson, Tennessee*

## Swap and You Shall *Receive*

DURING THE Korean War I was serving in the Navy aboard a ship docked in Philadelphia, getting ready to sail to the West Coast. Our captain had divided holiday shore leave into three shifts: Christmas, New Year's and the week after. I drew the first leave. However, there was a man in my division who was married with two kids. He drew the last shift. I was single. How could I let this man miss Christmas with his family? I asked my division officer if he'd allow a swap. He said okay, so I asked the man to switch. That was one happy guy!

I spent the holidays on duty. Finally, in January, I hopped on a southbound bus to visit my dad in Atlanta.

The bus made a stop in Charlotte, North Carolina. After picking up passengers, it left the station and was about to turn out onto the street when the driver's radio squawked. "Wait, you have one

PHOTOS BY PETER LAMASTRO

# Ways

more rider," came the dispatcher's voice.

A pretty little woman came running up, her arms full of packages. "You're lucky, ma'am," the bus driver said. "Another minute, and you would have had to get the next bus."

The woman stepped on, dropping some of her packages. There was an empty seat next to me and I told her I would hold her things so she could sit down. We talked the whole way. Her name was Johnnie. She was from Spartanburg and went to nursing school in Charlotte. She was going home for a weekend visit.

The next day, I couldn't stop talking about her. "Why are you staying here," my dad asked, "when your mind's in Charlotte?"

Good point. I spent the rest of my leave with Johnnie—and a bit more. When I got back to the ship I had to pay for it, but I didn't mind. After the war, I married that little woman. We spent 44 happy years together before she passed, had two kids, two grandkids and eight great-grandkids. All due to the Christmas I gave up, and the one minute God gave me in return.

*James Autry*
*Ludington, Michigan*

## The *Star* of the Show

Guideposts Classic 1987

GIAN CARLO Menotti's opera *Amahl and the Night Visitors* tells the mythical story of a visit by the Wise Men to a crippled shepherd boy named Amahl. In the dress rehearsal for our church production, try as we might, we couldn't get the star of Bethlehem to shine properly. When the stage lights hit it, the audience was almost blinded. Down it came to be spray-painted. Up it went, only to appear too dull. Down it came again to be covered with gold foil, spray-painted, then splattered with glue and glitter. Up it went a third time and from my position in the lighting booth, it finally looked right.

On opening night, I put on my headset to call out cues to the crew backstage. "Curtain up...begin!" Things went well until Amahl sang to his mother, begging her to let him stay outside a little longer. Suddenly it started raining—no, snowing—big chunks of gold from the Christmas star. Glitter and spray paint fell, revealing the gold foil underneath, making it shine brighter and brighter.

Amahl sang to his mother, "There is a star as large as a window," but, following the script, she refused to believe him.

"Amahl, when will you stop telling lies?" The audience, shielding their eyes from the glare, tittered. Anybody could see that star!

"Debbi," I heard the stage manager say in my headset, "I can't keep that star from shining." And in that unexpected moment, Christmas arrived for me. *I can't keep that star from shining.* Of course. No one can.

*Deborah Smoot*
*Salt Lake City, Utah*

Read more chill-down-your-spine stories at **guideposts.org/mysteriousways**

PETER LAMASTRO

# The Joy of Children

*"...and sleepless children's hearts are glad."*

—Sir John Betjeman

The Joy of Children

# The Christmas House

## What we lacked in money we made up for in imagination

**by Jan Goggans, Athens, Georgia**

CHRISTMAS WAS only a week away and my husband, Gary, and I still had no idea where we were going to find money to get presents for our children. Standing at the stove in my raggedy blue pajamas and fuzzy fuchsia socks I wondered what had happened to that high-earning buyer of designer clothing I used to be. The woman who took trips to New York City to see plays, try out trendy restaurants and spend the night in swanky hotels. *She bought a rundown farmhouse in the country,* I reminded myself. *And she quit her job to homeschool five kids!*

I didn't regret any of it, of course. Gary and I loved the outdoors and our old house overflowing with children and pets. But recent repairs and home additions had wiped out our funds. Gary's income wasn't enough to cover Christmas this year.

I herded the kids into the parlor for the day's lessons. Emory, 11, took a seat next to 9-year-old Avie. Five-year-old Archer held his little sister, Lily, while baby Burl crawled around on the floor between them. "I want to be an angel in our Christmas play," Avie reminded us. "And I'm going to pray that Lily can be one too."

"I want to be a Jedi knight in the play," said Archer.

"There were no Jedi knights at the manger," said Emory.

"There could be," said Archer.

How utterly different Archer's ideas about Christmas were from my own! Where I worried that I didn't have enough money to make Christmas happen, Archer thought anything was possible. If he could imagine a Jedi in the Christmas pageant, why couldn't it happen? It was that imagination that made the Christmas story real for him.

"Archer reminded me of a good spelling word," I said, signaling the start of school. "*Imagination*. Do you know what that is?"

"It's like pretending," said Avie.

"That's right," I said.

"I'm going to pretend to be an angel," said Lily. She had been practicing the role for days. She may have only been a little girl floating around the house in a white nightgown, but in her head Lily was an angel just like Archer was a Jedi. Did I ever have an imagination like that?

ILLUSTRATION BY DAVE CALVER

*Yes, I did,* I thought. A memory popped into my mind. "When I was little my brother, sister and I used to play in our father's toolshed," I told the kids. "Some days we imagined it was a castle, some days it was a country store, a hospital or a spaceship!" Archer made a blasting-off noise and practiced his new word. It had been years since I'd thought of that old shed. I could almost see it in my mind now—along with the castle, the hospital and the spaceship. Anything was possible for me then, especially at Christmas. Had I outgrown that kind of faith?

I THOUGHT ABOUT that toolshed all day, watching my own children play. If Archer could battle aliens in his bedroom and turn his baby brother into a Wookiee, surely I could find what I needed for a special Christmas in this house. At sunset I looked out the window and noticed one of the cats climbing on a pile of lumber left over from the construction on the house. That wood suddenly looked like the answer to my prayers.

"How about building a playhouse for the kids?" I asked Gary that night. "We've got the wood."

A grin broke out on his face. "I know a good carpenter. He might be willing to take on a day's work for me. But he'd have to do it on Christmas Eve to make it a surprise."

*Impossible,* I thought. No one would do that. I reminded myself that on Christmas anything was possible. "Call him," I said.

Two days before Christmas Gary took the kids off to their grandparents. The next morning a carpenter's truck rolled up to the house. Four men climbed out. "We can't afford a whole team!" I said.

"Don't worry," the one in charge told me. "We're helping out for free."

Volunteering on Christmas Eve? Now I knew this playhouse was God's idea. He had always had a soft spot for carpenters!

With the sound of saws, hammers and drills filling the air I went to my sewing room and got to work on princess dresses for Avie and Lily and Jedi-knight capes for Emory and Archer. By day's end the kids had a whole new costume wardrobe—and a new playhouse. It looked better than I had ever imagined: tin roof, fitted windows, white wooden door with a painted G, for Goggans, hanging over it.

Now to smuggle the kids back home without them noticing their Christmas present. To keep them from looking when they got near the house Gary scattered some candy on the floor of the car. Then he herded them inside, talking a mile a minute to distract them. Success!

The next morning I awoke before sunrise. I put luminaria all along the path to the playhouse. I set two old kerosene lamps on the table inside with a music box between them. A friendly glow shone through the windows. I went to fetch the troops.

"Ready?" asked Gary. Burl lay in his arms. The other children were already dressed and waiting behind him, bouncing up and down with excitement.

"Ready."

Gary opened the front door.

"Look at the lights!" Archer cried.

"Where do they go?" said Emory.

Gary led the way. The children gasped as the little house came into view. I opened the door and flipped open the music box. "Away in a manger, no crib for a bed..."

For a moment no one could speak. Then Lily clapped her hands for attention. "Our Christmas house," she announced.

"Oh, Mama," Avie said solemnly, "I'll remember this Christmas all my life!"

So would I. Who could forget the Christmas when a little imagination and a lot of faith created something out of nothing? And proved anything was possible.

Guideposts Classic 2005

# Daily Guideposts

*"Blessed is he that waiteth..."*
—Daniel 12:12

I thought I knew about waiting. Especially December waiting. I waited in line at the post office to mail my Christmas packages. I waited my turn at the florist's. And I waited to open that big package under the tree with my name on it. But last year's Advent season was different. Our daughter, Amy Jo, was going to have a December baby, and waiting took on a whole new intensity.

As her time got closer, we all went on "baby standby." If I didn't hear from Amy Jo by the end of each day, I called her. I started charging my cell phone, carrying it with me and actually turning it on—three things I seldom did before baby standby. I bought and wrapped my presents early. I saved up my vacation days at work. I made sure the car had a full tank of gas. And I waited—in a more heightened state of anticipation than any I could remember experiencing, even during my own pregnancies. And on December 22, when Amy Jo gave birth to a healthy baby boy, I knew it had been well worth the wait!

This Advent, I want to remember that expectancy, the happy hope embodied in the waiting. I want to realize that this year—and always and forever—a Child is born. But only if I'm on baby standby can I really know the joy his coming brings. Only if I'm watching with breathless longing will I find my waiting rewarded with a fresh sense of wonder, with a heightened awareness of love. With *Christmas*!

*I praise you, Father, for the miracle of birth, and the miracle of your love made flesh to dwell among us. I wait for your coming. Welcome, welcome, welcome, Baby Jesus!*

—Mary Lou Carney

DEBORAH ORY

# Puppy-in-the-Box

## My kids were getting older. Was there any way to reclaim the magic of Christmas?

**by Sarah Miller, Ridgefield, Connecticut**

LATE CHRISTMAS EVE, my two children were fast asleep. Even my husband, Evan, had turned in nearly an hour before. But I was still downstairs, arranging and rearranging the packages under the tree. No matter how I stacked them I couldn't get them the way I wanted. When the kids were small Christmas Eve was filled with so much anticipation. I couldn't wait to see the excitement in their faces the next morning as they tore through the wrapping paper to see what Santa had left them. But now they were growing up. It seemed nothing amazed them anymore. So this year I had arranged for a really big surprise. A surprise I now worried wasn't such a good idea. *Lord,* I wondered, *have I made a terrible mistake?*

PHOTOS BY PETER LAMASTRO

I glanced at the sugar cookies, the glass of milk and the carrots that we always left on the end table for Saint Nick. I remembered all the Christmas mornings Aaron and Audra had taken the missing treats as absolute proof Santa had visited. Now the kids played along with the cookie game more out of tradition than belief. Long gone were the days when LEGO sets and baby dolls set off shrieks of joy and the story of Jesus' birth was still new and suspenseful to them. Was that why I'd decided to surprise them with a puppy this year? Was it just me wanting to recapture that excitement? All I knew was our new dog would be here in a few hours. I hoped it would bring some of that old magic with it.

I had gotten the idea of getting a dog on the first day of school. I'd just put Audra on the bus when a woman came by walking a sheltie.

"What a beautiful dog," I said.

"Thanks," she replied. Then her voice lowered, like she was letting me in on a secret: "She's having puppies in a couple of months. Would you like one?"

"I'd *love* one," I said. The words flew out of my mouth. Then I hesitated. "But I'd better check with my husband first."

"I hope you told her no," Evan said that evening when I told him. "We don't have the room or the money for a dog."

I knew he was right. We already had a cat and two guinea pigs. But still...

"Can't you just see the kids getting a puppy for Christmas?" I said.

The puppies were born in early November. I went over to see them one morning right after I got the kids off to school.

There in a small pen was the mother dog nursing six tiny little things. They looked more like rats than dogs, but they were beautiful all the same. "Would you like to hold one?" the breeder asked. How could I say no? I held a squirming ball of fur against my face and he softly kissed my cheek with his tongue. I felt a tingle all over, like when the kids rushed downstairs to their presents. "You would be the best Christmas present ever," I said as I returned him to his pen. In early December I took Evan to see the puppies and he gave in to my pleas.

But now I was having misgivings. *The kids are growing up,* I thought as I headed up to bed. *I can't turn back the clock. And a dog isn't going to bring back the old magic.* It seemed forever before I drifted to sleep.

I awoke to shrieks of "Merry Christ-

**LET IT BARK!** *Aaron and Audra love Rusty.*

**DOGSLEDDING**
*Rusty has become part of the family.*

mas!" Audra climbed under the covers next to me. Aaron pushed in beside Evan. "Can we open the presents?" they shouted. The kids were in their Christmas jammies. Evan and I got on our robes. I made coffee and we headed down to the family room and the tree.

Audra's eyes went from the presents to the half-eaten cookies. "He was here all right, Mommy," she said.

"Yes, dear," I said. Maybe Audra was humoring me, but she was still a great kid. *Lord, I should be grateful for the blessings you give me,* I thought, and handed Aaron a present.

Aaron unwrapped the bowling ball and shoes we'd gotten him. He'd joined a league that fall.

"Cool!" he said. "It's blue, just like I wanted. Thanks, Mom and Dad." Audra was ripping the paper off her Barbie Beetle when there was a knock on the door.

My heart skipped a beat. It was my big Christmas surprise. Suddenly I felt silly. Did the kids even want a puppy? "Who could that be?" I managed to get out. "Stay here and I'll go check."

I ran up the stairs and opened the front door. "Merry Christmas," the breeder said. "And good luck." I put the puppy inside a big box I'd wrapped in green and red paper, then put the lid on top of it. Immediately he started whimpering. *Maybe I shouldn't bother with the package,* I thought. But since I'd already gone to the trouble.... "Shhh," I whispered. "It's only for a moment.

"Kids! Come look!" I cried out. "Santa just left another pres—"

They were there before I could get the words out of my mouth, Evan right behind them. The lid inched upward on the box and I gently held it in place. "What is it?" Audra gasped. She was shaking she was so excited.

"I don't know," I said. "Let's find out."

Ever so slowly Audra lifted the lid. "It's a puppy!" she screamed. *Arf,* the little dog barked. Audra snatched him out of the box and held him tight against her chest. He licked her face. Audra squealed.

"What do you think we should name him?" I asked.

"He has a bit of reddish brown on his nose," Aaron said, reaching over Audra to pet the little guy's head. His eyes were shining. "I think we should call him Rusty."

I looked over at Evan, but he only had eyes for the puppy. And he'd known about the surprise all along. That's when I realized I was grinning too. Grinning from ear to ear, like a kid on...

"This is the best Christmas ever," Audra said. I agreed. *Thank you, Lord.* I'd thought the years of magical Christmas mornings were over. All it took to bring them back was one small puppy. Turns out you're never too old to believe in the magic of Christmas.

# The *Gift* of Time

## A granddaughter and a lesson learned

**by Nancy Bowser, Roanoke, Virginia**

ONE THING I've never had enough of at Christmas is time. I'd spent the previous few days running around buying presents, trimming the tree, decorating the house. The whole family was going to be there. Even my 87-year-old mother was coming from the nursing home. I wanted everything to be perfect. I picked Mom up in the early afternoon and settled her wheelchair in the family room where the tree was. No sooner had I sat down to talk to her than the doorbell rang. One by one, family members trickled into the house. Uncles, cousins, aunts. "Merry Christmas, Grandma," my 11-year-old granddaughter, Laura, said. "I can't wait to tell you what happened at school yesterday."

"I would love to hear it," I replied. "But I don't have time right now."

I ran back and forth between the door and the kitchen, setting out cookies and adjusting the decorations. When I finally took a break to enjoy the house, filled with laughter and delicious smells, I realized I'd forgotten all about Mom!

I rushed to the family room. I expected to find Mom sitting by herself. Instead I found Laura on the floor at her feet. "And then my teacher said I'd gotten all the answers right," she was saying. "School has been so great this year. Do you want to hear about my favorite class?"

The lights on my perfect Christmas tree looked paltry in comparison with the brightness in my mother's eyes as she talked with Laura. Time seemed to stand still while I watched them. In all my rushing around I'd forgotten why everyone got together in the first place. Decorations and presents were nice, but they weren't as important as spending time with loved ones. Laura and Mom knew that. I was sure, finally, that I knew it too.

ILLUSTRATION BY SYLVIE DAIGNAULT

# They Call Me "The Toy Guy"

## Who says play is just for kids?

**by Chris Byrne, New York, New York**

I GET paid to play, and if you ask me, Matchbox cars were the best toy ever made. I was convinced of that as a child. Opening up my plastic carrying case in my room just before Christmas, I saw endless possibilities. Would I pretend the flaming red race car had the power to fly through space? Or crash it into the blue pickup truck?

What was it that made Matchbox cars so much fun? Those little metal cars could *do* anything and *be* anything. I threw myself into those adventures the same way I threw myself into the stories I learned in Sunday school or our yearly Christmas pageant. I was an ordinary boy, but when I put on my costume and stepped onstage, I was a shepherd tending his flock on the very first Christmas. Standing there with my lamb beside me, I felt the excitement and fear the real shepherds must have felt that night. Maybe all that practice stretching my mind around fantastic ideas helped me open my heart to the true wonders of Christmas. What had happened in Bethlehem was more amazing than any flying space car—and yet it had really happened. Real life had trumped anything I could dream up!

That gave me the answer to a problem I had the Christmas I was eight: What should I ask Santa for this year? My parents were teachers raising five kids, and as Mom always said, Santa only had so much room on his sleigh. I couldn't get everything I wanted. What toy should I choose? The Thimble City, I decided, pulling out paper to write my letter. Like my Matchbox cars, the three-square-foot city with people, cars and plastic buildings could be anything and everything.

Christmas morning my Thimble City was waiting. By Christmas night that city had been attacked by monsters, invaded by aliens and had put on its own Christmas pageant.

That kind of play comes naturally to children, so I thought I'd have to give it up as I got older. As a teenager I didn't play with my Matchbox cars, but I still liked to open the case and remind myself to be open to amazing things. I even took them with me to college, where I studied theater. As an actor I would be able to use my imagination every day! Being a Broadway star would be like playing with toys again, a dream come true.

"Why'd you bring those?" my roommate

asked, laughing, when I set the Matchbox case on the shelf.

"I just don't like my brothers messing with my stuff," I mumbled. I couldn't tell my roommate the real reason I'd brought them, that no matter how old I got those cars were a reminder of the fantastic things that could happen when God was working in the world.

Reality didn't always match my dreams. After graduation I moved to New York City. No big breaks on Broadway for me. I got a job editing textbooks that eventually led me to marketing and the toy business. It turned out grown-ups *can* play with toys—and even earn a living by reviewing them. Today I'm director of content for **timetoplaymag.com**. I've appeared on the *Today* show and *Live! with Regis and Kelly* and talked about toys on National Public Radio. They call me the Toy Guy. I love that! Once again God showed me that real life could be more fantastic than my dreams.

**SANTA'S HELPER** *Chris and a few of his favorite things*

The Toy Guy talks about the value of play, how toys inspire kids and trends this holiday season at **guideposts.org/chrisbyrne**

PETER LAMASTRO

# One Christmas in New York

by Edward Grinnan, Editor-in-Chief, GUIDEPOSTS, and author of *The Promise of Hope*

UNTIL THAT YEAR I had hardly ever missed going home to see my family for Christmas. Only once before, in fact, when, right after college, I was trekking in the Peruvian Andes during a fairly improvisational journey to parts more or less unknown. That year, my mother later told me, most of the discussion around the holiday table was about when they'd ever see me again. "We had no idea," she told me later, "because you didn't call." Did I mention that my mother was a bit of a worrier? I called her a prayer worrier rather than a prayer warrior.

Truth was that now, at age 30, I had given her more to worry and pray about than any loving mother ever deserved. A reckless, artistic and footloose youth had transmogrified into something much darker and more disturbing than my mother knew. And this Christmas, 1983, two weeks after I turned 30, I had to tell my mother I wasn't coming home. That coming home was too dangerous. At least for me. At least for now.

"If you get on a plane for Detroit, Edward," my sponsor in the 12-step program I'd joined warned me, "you might not make it back. The holidays can be tough. Everyone will be toasting and celebrating. That's fine for most folks, but for people like us it's a matter of life and death. It's your first Christmas sober…your first month, actually. You should stick close to your meetings. You need all the support you can get right now."

Of that I had no doubt. I was on shaky ground. In the years since I had finished graduate school and drifted down from

JEFFERSON HAYMAN/CORBIS

## My sobriety was still fragile, but I found strength in family—old and new

New Haven to New York, alcohol had subsumed my life like some treacherous rip current I kept getting caught in. I'd been in enough trouble at school, taking four years to complete a three-year master of fine arts program. Even then I spent my final semester living at the student health center so I could be supervised and medicated.

New York and its environs were altogether a more dangerous game. The girl I'd moved here with from New Haven quickly left me...and I couldn't blame her. If I could have left me I would have. But that was the problem. I'd walk past the huge churches and cathedrals in this great city and cry out for help, but no answer ever came except the plaintive echo of my own dissolute voice.

Finally, on a cold, rainy day in the East Village, an old friend smacked me over the head with one of those cheapo street umbrellas until she got me to a 12-step meeting on Perry Street. Yes, it was grim and crowded and the man talking was clearly nearing the final stages of AIDS. My mind said, *Why bother to stop now, dude? Go out in style.* Yet even as I thought it I couldn't help but grasp the courage of a dying man who wanted to meet his Lord sober.

I was introduced to others and everyone was eager to give me their phone numbers. Since I didn't have a phone, that seemed pointless...until a collection was taken and I was awarded a wealth of coins to use at pay phones. "No excuses now," someone said.

For the past month I'd trudged to meetings once, twice, three times a day. I turned 30 in a huge "sober party" that was as wild and fun as anything I'd ever done. As

Christmas neared, though, I pined for home, for the beautiful clean snow of Michigan and midnight Mass with my family at St. Owen's. What I wouldn't have given to be back there with them, like it was before everything had gone so wrong in my life. There wasn't anything about my family that was bad for me. I came from a good family and they were supporting me in my decision to play it safe this year. There would be plenty of time to go home later when I had a few stable months under my belt.

> **I stopped to admire the holiday windows: Santa's workshop, the elves still working furiously even at this late hour. I shivered and watched, feeling lonelier and lonelier.**

Which was why I found myself wandering alone down a quiet Fifth Avenue late on Christmas Eve. There was a fresh dusting of snow on the sidewalk and the buildings soared into a frozen sky. Only the brightest stars shone through the ambient light. All I had on was a raincoat with no lining, and I shivered when I stopped to admire the holiday windows at Lord & Taylor: Santa's workshop, the elves still working furiously even at this late hour. I watched, feeling lonelier and lonelier. A figure passed me and turned—a woman named Casey from one of my meetings. She was older than me and had been sober a while.

"Where are you off to?" I asked.

"Midnight Mass. Want to come?"

I joined her and in a few minutes we were inside the church, edging our way up the side of the sanctuary until we could find a decent place to stand since the pews were packed. Crowded, just like everything else in New York. But warm, too, especially when the choir lifted its voice in "O Come, All Ye Faithful"!

We'd pushed up next to a side altar that had been converted to a crèche. A beautiful Mary, the most beautiful Mary figurine I had ever seen, knelt lovingly over the Baby Jesus in his crib. Joseph stood above her, his hand resting tenderly on her shoulder. There were others around too, shepherds and animals. But my attention was riveted on the three gorgeous figures and all that the humble scene proclaimed. *You,* I thought, *you are my family tonight.*

After Mass Casey took me to an all-night coffee shop on Third Avenue open even on Christmas Eve, where a bunch of people I knew from meetings in the neighborhood were drinking coffee, singing carols and generally having a fine Christmas time. Someone bought me breakfast, which tasted better than anything I'd ever eaten, probably because I hadn't eaten in a while. We stayed until the sun came up over the East River on Christmas morn. I went home to change clothes and get ready for another meeting. But not before I found a phone and called home to let them know I was okay.

It was a few more years still before I found my way, and when I did I found my way to GUIDEPOSTS and another kind of family, the family of GUIDEPOSTS and its readers. But each Christmas in New York, where I still live and work not far from that church, I always remember the one family I am never far from and who will be there always.

Guideposts Classic 2003

# Daily Guideposts

*"And the Lord direct your hearts into the love of God, and into the patient waiting for Christ."* —II Thessalonians 3:5

Every year I've promised myself that I'd go back to my boarding school, Hoosac, and see the Christmas celebration that's been held there for 108 years. This year, I kept my promise. I went, dreading the changes I'd find. The campus had been moved to a nearby hill, presided over by the baronial Tebutt mansion. I was accustomed to the school anthem, which began *Oculos meos levavi* ("I will lift up mine eyes," Psalm 121:1), and it was to that hill we had lifted them up.

"You're here at last," said headmaster Richard Lomuscio warmly when I arrived, and after meeting with other alumni, we walked to the dining hall for the ceremony. I knew from the sight of two Beefeaters standing rigidly at the entrance that all would be well. It was. First came the boar's head, borne on a trencher, followed by Christmas delicacies, and then the deeply reverent homage to the Christ Child. After dinner, we were ready for Elizabethan merriment. The Yule log was rolled in, and everyone in the hall enjoyed the stately sword dance, the troubadours, the mummers' play—everything that I remembered. Tradition held.

The next morning I went to find the old campus. All the buildings save one were gone. A tangle of trees and brush had taken over. I turned to the surviving structure, the old stone chapel. I felt a pang of memory and then a presentiment, something good. Here was where I had gained my first appreciation of God. Here was where the students worshipped. What could be better than that? And so you see, tradition held.

*There's an inscription on the mantel of the fireplace where the Yule log blazed, the mantel brought up from the old campus. The words are about you, Father:* Deus Regit *("God Reigns").*

—Van Varner

DEBORAH ORY

# Mysterious

## A *Dream* House Come True

I WHEELED my shopping cart through Toys "R" Us, picking up some last-minute gifts for my two girls. I pulled out my list—almost every item was checked off. Last thing? A Barbie horse and carriage. *Boy, that Barbie has everything!* I thought. I turned down the pink and white Barbie aisle and came face-to-face with a large display: Barbie Dream Houses. My heart sank. Barbie might have it all, but those houses reminded me of one little girl who didn't.

My extended family had decided that Christmas to help out a young single mother struggling to raise her four children. We asked the mother to write down the necessities for each child and one small toy. My family was assigned the eight-year-old girl. My daughters and I had a blast picking out the winter clothes and boots the mother had requested. But at the bottom of the list, the child had asked for a Barbie Dream House. Three stories, lights and sounds, a working elevator. The cost was over my budget.

Still, I knew how much joy my own girls got from such things. *Lord, my children are so blessed,* I prayed. *I'd love this little girl to have something special this Christmas.*

I headed for the checkout. The wait seemed like forever. Finally, a cashier opened a new line and waved me over. I put the horse and carriage on the conveyor belt.

"Could you wait just a moment?" the cashier asked. She walked over to a man who looked like the manager. They chatted for a minute. What was going on? The cashier returned. "How would you like a free Barbie Dream House?" she asked.

"What?" I could barely speak. "How..."

"We had a special promotion a few months ago," the cashier explained, "where you could get a Barbie Dream House free. I just got the feeling I should ask my manager about it."

I knew that feeling exactly.

*Suzanne Boatright*
*Carmel, Indiana*

## Angel at the *Wheel*

Guideposts Classic 2005

DRIVING HOME from a visit to my family for Christmas, I came to a two-lane road where traffic was slow but steady. A fine mist saturated the cold air and the highway was growing slick.

Suddenly my wheels skidded and the brakes locked. The guardrail was coming up fast!

I cried out, "God, help me!" The impact of the crash threw me over the seat and I blacked out.

I woke up on the floor in the backseat. A man and a boy were bent over me. "You hit a patch of ice," the man said. "A policeman saw the whole thing. He's radioing for help."

Peering out the window, I realized that

PHOTOS BY PETER LAMASTRO

# Ways

my car had been moved to the opposite side of the highway and parked safely on the grass off the shoulder. *How in the world did I get over here?* Before I could ask, another car hit the same patch of ice and spun into the guardrail—at the exact spot I had. The man and his son ran to help.

When trucks arrived to sand the road, father and son returned with the policeman. "By the way," the policeman said, "what happened to your companion?"

I looked at him quizzically: "Who?"

"He drove your car to this spot," the officer said. "I saw him."

"We saw him too," said the father. "He crossed the lane of oncoming traffic and parked right here. But no one got out. In fact, we had to break a window to get in."

There had been no man in my car. But Someone had been with me.

*Dorothy Howard*
*Amherst, Massachusetts*

## Let It *Snow!*

Guideposts Classic 1988

IN SEPTEMBER Sister Grace began forming a picture of a Christmas tree in her mind. As the director of pastoral care at Charleston's St. Francis Xavier Hospital, Sister Grace had been asked to decorate the tree that would be placed in the lobby of the Omni Hotel. The tree she envisioned would have angels on it and snowflakes—lots of snowflakes, exquisite ones crocheted by hand. By Thanksgiving Sister Grace had acquired the angels, but the snowflakes were not to be found.

On the day before Thanksgiving, Doris Hartvig was admitted to the hospital for tests. Doris detested idleness, and she was soon busy at work with a hook and yarn.

"Could you do a snowflake?" one of the nuns, Sister Mary Joseph, asked her.

"I can," Doris replied. In fact, not long before, she had bought a book with instructions on how to crochet snowflakes. They weren't easy to make, and each one required a lot of time. With renewed hope, Sister Grace went to see Doris. She described in detail the Christmas tree she had her heart set on, with a blue bow on top, angels clinging to the branches and lacy snowflakes hanging from the boughs.

"How many snowflakes do you need?" Doris finally asked.

"We should have sixty," Sister Grace replied, "but there's no time to make that many."

Doris smiled. She reached under her bed and took out a bag of needlework, and then drew out one beautiful crocheted snowflake after another—40, 50, over 60 of them! They were ironed, starched and ready to be hung.

In September Doris Hartvig had felt a great and seemingly inexplicable urge to crochet snowflakes. Now she knew why.

*Robert Hawkins*
*St. Johns Island, South Carolina*

Read more chill-down-your-spine stories at **guideposts.org/mysteriousways**

PETER LAMASTRO

# The Joy of Miracles

*"This wondrous miracle did Love devise..."*

*—Sir John Davies*

ILLUSTRATION BY PENELOPE DULLAGHAN

# Heavenly Music

## Christmas wouldn't be Christmas without carols. Here's an amazing story about where an all-time favorite came from

**by Richard W. O'Donnell, Port Richey, Florida**

Guideposts Classic 1999

ON A BRIGHT spring morning in 1854, Ludwig Eck sat down to breakfast in a quaint Prussian inn near the Austrian border.

As master of the Royal Court Choir in Berlin, Eck had been given a special task: track down the composer of the favorite hymn of the King of Prussia, Friedrich Wilhelm IV. Though "The Song From Heaven" was known all over the continent, it had no attribution in the songbooks. "I must know the composer's name!" declared the king.

Eck traveled across Prussia and neighboring countries on horseback. He investigated every rumor, and even rumors of rumors, that came his way about "The Song From Heaven." The search had exhausted him, and he had neglected his work as concertmaster. After seven years, he was still no closer to finding out who wrote the heavenly music so beloved by the king. He was just returning from yet another failed attempt. Eck tried to concentrate on the meal before him, but the thought of again disappointing His Majesty ruined his appetite.

Reaching for his coffee, Eck heard an all-too-familiar melody being whistled in the air above him. The king's hymn? He wondered if, after all this time, he had begun humming the tune without even knowing it. Nevertheless, he twisted around in his chair and slowly raised his eyes toward the ceiling. The sound did seem to be coming from above his head.

There Eck noticed for the first time a wrought-iron cage holding a little black-and-red bird—a bullfinch, if he wasn't mistaken. The bird was sitting on its perch, happily singing. Eck cocked his ear toward the cage. Could it be true? This delightful creature was serenading him with the very song he had been searching for.

*He cocked an ear toward the sound. Could it be true? This delightful creature was serenading him with the very song he had been searching for!*

Across the room, the waiter noticed the expression on Eck's face. He hurried to the table. "Shall I remove the bird, sir?" the waiter asked.

"That song!" Eck nearly shouted. "The bird is singing the king's favorite hymn. Please tell me where that bird came from."

"I will check with the innkeeper," the waiter offered, and rushed off to find the owner.

Eck pushed away the buttered rolls and marmalade. He was too excited to eat. He drummed his fingers on the table, the bird warbling all the while. Finally the waiter returned.

"Yes?" Eck asked eagerly.

"The bullfinch was purchased from young Felix Gruber, a student at St. Peter's Abbey across the Austrian border." Eck shook the waiter's hand and got up from the table. No time for breakfast now. Within the hour, Eck's horse was ready, and he was on his way to the abbey in Salzburg. The abbot at St. Peter's was not pleased to hear about the bird. "I am not in favor of caging one of God's creatures," he said.

"If you'll pardon me, I must speak to Felix Gruber," said the concertmaster. "I am here on His Majesty's business." The abbot sniffed, then nodded to his assistant.

Minutes later the 15-year-old boy was brought before Eck. "Yes, sir," the boy said, eyeing the abbot nervously, "I caught the bullfinch and taught it to sing the song."

"Who taught *you* the song, young man?"

"My father," said the youth. Eck grew impatient. The father had, no doubt, learned it from someone else, and so on down the line. Eck would visit each person named, and in the end wind up where he had started—with no idea who had created the melody.

"And where did your father learn the song?" Eck asked halfheartedly.

"My father," said Felix Gruber with a trace of pride, "did not have to learn that song. He wrote the music. And his friend Father Josef Mohr wrote the words."

The concertmaster almost leaped with joy, but he was far too dignified. "I would be honored to meet Herr Gruber," Eck said. "I have waited a long time."

One week later Eck arrived in the Austrian village of Hallein, where the elder Gruber was the organist at the local church. "Yes, I wrote the music," Franz Gruber said, surprised to be receiving a visit from the Royal Concertmaster himself. Eck pressed him: When? Where? Under what circumstances? For a specific occasion? Eck wanted all the details for the king.

Gruber obliged. "In 1818, I was the organist at St. Nicholas's Church in Oberndorf," he began. "When the organ broke down on Christmas Eve, it seemed we would not have any music at our Christmas service. Father Mohr had written a poem about the birth of Christ. At his request, I immediately put music to the words. I had never worked so fast in all my life. But I was pleased with the result and performed it on guitar at midnight Mass."

The organ at St. Nicholas continued to break down. Since it could only be properly fixed by the itinerant repairman who came once every spring, it seemed the old instrument was broken more often than not. Finally, years after Gruber's midnight guitar performance on Christmas Eve, the church commissioned a man named Carl Mauracher to build a brand-new organ. While he was working in the choir loft, he came across a handwritten copy of Gruber's song and took the sheet music back to his home in the Ziller Valley. Soon people were singing the song at Christmastime throughout the Tyrolean mountains. From there, the song spread.

"The song is known all over Europe," Eck informed the composer.

"Is it?" Gruber said, surprised.

Eck smiled at the organist. "That is why I have searched seven years for you, sir," he said. "The King of Prussia has been waiting a long time to know the composer of 'The Song From Heaven.'"

Gruber was puzzled. "'The Song From Heaven'?"

"That is what people call your song in Europe," the concertmaster explained. "What do you call it?"

"We call it by the title of Father Mohr's poem," said Gruber. "We call it 'Silent Night.'"

Eck was anxious to report to the king, but on the way back to Berlin he made a quick stop. "A successful journey?" the waiter asked when Eck entered the dining room at the inn near the border.

"Yes, thank you," Eck replied. "But I have one more request." He pricked his ears for the bird's song. "I would like to buy the bullfinch."

The innkeeper agreed, and Eck asked if the songbird had been named. It had not. "I'll take care of that!" Eck said, carrying the bird home with him to Berlin.

With his quest finally over, Eck resumed his duties with the Royal Choir and devoted himself to making music once more.

King Friedrich Wilhelm IV never forgot the good work his concertmaster had done. Year-round the bullfinch serenaded Eck with "Silent Night." During the part where "heavenly hosts sing hallelujah," Eck imagined his songbird among them. For he had named his winged messenger Angel. It was she who had heralded the end of his journey.

Watch a video of our staff's rendition of "Deck the Halls" at **guideposts.org/deckthehalls**

# Salvation Army Angel

## She came to lift my sorrows

**by Kathy Judy, Altoona, Pennsylvania**

I LOVED Christmas. The joy of the season, the lights and carols, the old family ornaments on the tree. This year, though, two weeks before the holiday, driving through traffic to buy gifts for my family, I was struggling not to cry. *Think of your grandsons,* I told myself. But try as I might, I couldn't keep the sad reality of my life from intruding into my thoughts. "Please, Lord," I whispered, from the depths of my soul, "help lift my sorrows."

A bad relationship with my landlord—my ex-husband's mother—had recently forced me from the home I'd lived in for decades. I'd only been able to take with me some clothes, a few possessions and my black Lab before the locks were changed. I didn't want to burden my family with my problems, but on my teacher's salary and without time to search for a place of my own, I had no choice but to move in with my daughter Tina and her family. They cleared two attic rooms for me, with my bed, a dresser and a chair in one, and a cupboard and my computer in the other. I tried to keep to myself as much as I could. Still, it was a difficult situation that put undue stress on my daughter and son-in-law. I became increasingly depressed. I felt all alone with my sorrows.

The one bright spot was my grandkids. Seven-year-old Scott and five-year-old Kody were too young to understand what was happening to me. They just loved that I was now living with them. They snuck into the attic to visit, and I gave them cookies and treats. "You're spoiling them, Mom!" Tina would say. But she was grateful that something could still bring a smile to my face.

Only they could inspire me to leave the house on a night like this. It was threatening to snow, and the bitter cold seemed to seep into my bones. I wasn't looking forward to fighting the crowds in the stores. But I didn't want the boys to wake up Christmas morning to discover no presents from Grandma under the tree. I couldn't look into their eyes and tell them, "I'm sorry, guys, Grandma is too depressed. She couldn't think of anything to get you this year."

I headed to a shopping center. *Just a quick trip, in and out before the storm hits,* I thought. I parked in front of Value City. I didn't normally shop there, but it was convenient. It would have to do.

I found a space at the rear of the park-

ILLUSTRATION BY ROBERT HUNT

THE SALVATION ARMY

ing lot and walked toward the building. As I got closer, I heard the tinkle of a small bell. At the far left side of the entrance, I saw the source—a woman standing and waving a bell next to the distinctive red Salvation Army kettle.

She didn't look like any Salvation Army bell ringer I'd ever seen—no red apron, for starters. She wore an unusual large and downy white coat with a fluffy

*Kindness emanated from her, like the warm feeling you get from seeing a close friend you haven't seen in a while.*

white hood fitted around her face. She was exotic looking, with dark hair and crystal-clear light blue eyes. Her skin was smooth and unwrinkled. She smiled at me as I entered the store.

I GRABBED A CART and made my way up and down the aisles. Hot Wheels and coloring books for Scott and Kody. Sweaters for Tina and my other daughter, Heather. A colorful instrument that made different noises for Heather's baby. Kevin, my son-in-law, liked flannel shirts, and there was a nice selection. Each item I added to my cart seemed to take some weight off my shoulders. *Giving, that's what this season is about,* I thought. God gave us the greatest gift we ever could hope for, and Christmas was the time to show that same generosity—not to focus on our own problems.

I paid for my purchases and left, pushing the cart full of gifts out of the store. I again passed the Salvation Army worker. This time, her piercing blue eyes stopped me in my tracks. It was as if she could see right into my heart. Kindness emanated from her, like the warm feeling you get from seeing a close friend you haven't seen in a while. A light snow had begun to fall. I was anxious to get home, but I just stood there with my cart. I couldn't ignore the emotion that came over me. *You have some money left,* I thought. *Put it in the kettle. Help somebody else.*

I reached into my wallet, and took out all the bills I had. I dropped the money into the kettle. I looked into the woman's eyes. Time seemed to slow. Her fluffy white hood moved in the breeze, her ageless face lit up.

"The Lord has sent me to tell you that your sorrow has been lifted," she said.

How could she possibly know my prayer? Unless...I felt a warmth wash over my spirit, a peace inside me I hadn't felt for a long time. I somehow managed to murmur a thank-you.

In a daze, I walked back to my car, loaded it up and climbed inside. Only then did I have a moment to think about what the bell ringer had said. I looked back at her. Standing with her white coat and the snow swirling around her, she really did look as if she had angels' wings.

Shortly after that Christmas, my life began to change. Out walking my dog one day I spotted a house for rent three blocks away from Tina's. I inquired, and the rent was absurdly low, well within my budget. I still lived close enough for the grandkids to walk over for cookies and treats! Slowly I got to know a new neighbor, Paul. We've been married now for nearly 10 years.

Every morning, I fasten an angel pin to my clothing, to remind me of the mysterious bell ringer who encouraged me that snowy night. She showed me I wasn't alone with my sorrows. The Lord will help me shoulder my burdens, no matter how heavy they become.

# Hope's Blaze

## The fire that burned down our house transformed me...and something I loved

**by Julie Perkins, Steelville, Missouri**

SOME PEOPLE collect figurines. I love Nativity sets. When I was small, I would sit on the floor by the crèche and arrange the pieces—people and animals—to be sure each had an unobstructed view of the Baby Jesus. After all, he was the reason they gathered at the manger in the first place. Some had traveled many miles to see him—God's promise fulfilled.

Eventually, my collection grew so large, I had a set in every room of my house. My favorite was a small ceramic set made by my mother-in-law, each piece glazed a gleaming white.

Several years ago in February, my family and I returned from church to find our house in flames. There was no saving it. We lost everything and had to move into a camper. One morning I picked my way across the burned timbers and broken floors that had been our home. *Lord, let me find one thing I can salvage from this rubble.* What that might be, I couldn't fathom.

A large decorative tin stood out in the debris. I recognized it immediately. I'd wrapped some of my Nativity sets in newspaper and stored them inside. The tin was burned bare of color. I pried off the lid. *Oh, my Lord!* The newspaper wrappings had burned completely. Pieces lay jumbled inside. They were undamaged, but devoid of color. Every piece was dull, ship-primer gray. It was like the life had been sucked out of them. Looking at them, I felt the same way.

I was about to close the tin when I spotted a sliver of color at the bottom. It was my mother-in-law's set—now glazed in a variety of colors, from shiny gray to iron red. *The colors from the others must have bled into the white,* I thought.

I set the pieces from that set on the table of our camper. Of all the things I could have found, this was what I needed most. *The Lord's promise, his promise of new life.*

We rebuilt our house. I collected new Nativity sets. At Christmas when I arrange them, I take care with my old favorite, the one that survived the flames. For me it carries the Christmas message: The new life born in a stable 2,000 years ago is alive and well for us today. The promise that Christmas brings is indestructible. It is my strength all year round.

**FORGED BY FIRE**
*One of the figures from the Nativity set made by Julie's mother-in-law*

PETER LAMASTRO

# Have Yourself a *Thrift-Shop* Christmas

## Shopping on a budget can be fun

**by Nan Kennedy Morrison, Bartlesville, Oklahoma**

I'M A GIFT-GIVER. I always have been. Especially at Christmastime. There's nothing more exciting than shopping for the people I love, then watching them open the present that's perfect for them. But this year I was afraid there'd be no shopping.

It was a few weeks before Christmas and I sat at my kitchen table staring at my checkbook. Bills had left me with next to nothing in my gift budget. There were a dozen people on my list—my husband, Frank, our son, nieces, nephews, friends....

*I'll never be able to afford something for everyone,* I thought.

As usual, my faltering faith called my favorite Bible verse, Proverbs 3:5–6, to mind: "Trust in the Lord with all thine heart, and lean not unto thine own understanding; in all thy ways acknowledge him and he shall direct thy paths."

*Okay, Lord,* I prayed, *help me make this money stretch. I trust you.*

The newspaper was on the table next to me. I flipped through it, and an article about a weekend estate sale practically jumped off the page. *Maybe I'll check it out,* I thought, and wrote down the address. I turned the page. There, smack dab in the middle, was an ad for the Goodwill store. *Hmm, they might have a few things too.* On the next? A garage sale listing. After that, one for a thrift shop. "Okay, Lord, I'm listening," I said aloud. "Direct my path."

That weekend I drove over to the estate sale. First I browsed through the living room. There was antique furniture, tables crowded with vases and lamps. Nothing caught my eye. I walked over to an office area and looked at some electronics. Nothing there either. Another room had beautiful artwork, but everything was out of my price range. *Maybe this is a waste of time,* I thought, wandering into the kitchen. Bingo! A table loaded with lace handkerchiefs for a dollar apiece. My sister collected handker-

chiefs! And up high on a pantry shelf was a sealed exotic mustard made in Eufaula, Oklahoma, a small town near where we'd grown up. I knew she'd get a kick out of that. To cap it off, I added a brand-new, still-in-the-box crystal water pitcher.

The race was on! The next day I hit the Goodwill. I found a men's designer dress shirt in just the right size for my hard-to-fit son, still with original creases, for just a few dollars. A couple of days later I discovered a gorgeous choker with an unusual sapphire-colored stone in the center. Just the thing for my fashionista niece! Next up were the garage sales. There were two terrific finds for Frank: a CD of Oklahoma's centennial anniversary celebrations and a movie featuring Andy Griffith, his favorite actor.

"Have you bought anything for yourself?" Frank asked one afternoon when I came home with more packages. "Christmas is about other people," I said. But on my next trip to the thrift shop I found a rust-colored jacket that matched an outfit I had. Thanks to all the wonderful deals I'd found I had enough money to buy it along with two knit shirts with sleeves long enough to cover my nephew's basketball-reach arms and an evening purse for another niece. And the perfect finish to all of my great finds: a bag full of glittering red ribbons that made all those gifts look like I'd spent a fortune. By Christmas not only did I have special gifts for everyone on my list, but I had a few dollars out of my budget to spare. Those I donated to Samaritan's Purse—Franklin Graham's international relief charity.

My family all said the gifts I had given them were perfect.

"How did you know I'd like that?" they kept asking on Christmas Day. It was easy, I told them. God had directed my path.

ILLUSTRATION BY ROSS MACDONALD

# Tidings of Joy

## I am an archaeologist, used to making the unexplainable explainable, piecing together the past. But there was no obvious explanation for what happened to me that Christmas Eve as I lay near death in a hospital bed

**by Sal Trento, Venice, California**

Guideposts Classic 2006

IT WAS CHRISTMASTIME, and all around me I saw blinking red and green lights. But not the kind you want to see at Christmas. I saw these lights from a bed in intensive care, through a fog of pain and medication. As long as the lights kept blinking, I was alive. Yet at this juncture of my life I couldn't help asking myself, *What do I have to live for?*

I considered the facts. That, after all, is what I was trained to do. I was an archaeologist. I pieced together the histories of ancient peoples. I could tell the diet of a prehistoric Majorcan tribesman by analyzing a few fragments of teeth and bone. I might even be able to tell you what he died of. Now I tried to put together the pieces of my own life. What would some archaeologist of the future have to say about me? That I had died of injuries to my kidneys sustained in a car accident after my brand-new SUV spun out on a patch of black ice in the Colorado Rockies? That I left behind a wife and kids from whom I was estranged? That I'd cared more about the past than the present?

Which was why, perhaps, I had no visitors to my hospital room except for an unending parade of doctors, nurses and technicians, looking grim but determined to keep me alive as long as my battered kidneys managed to function. I'd been put in an ICU room right across from the nurses' station, so I could be watched more closely, just in case the lights stopped blinking.

*Merry Christmas, Sal,* I told myself. *It's probably your last.*

Not that Christmas meant much to me. At least not spiritually. I grew up going to church with my family on Christmas Eve. And with my own kids I always put up a tree and made sure there were presents under it. Otherwise it was all myth and ritual, like the ancient societies I studied.

"You care more about your work than me," my wife had said the night she announced she wanted a divorce. I couldn't argue with her. I spent months in far-flung places, like some modern-day Indiana Jones. To my wife I cared more about somebody's past than I did about our future. Yet now, clinging to life, I wanted to fight for that future.

But it was too late. The damage had been done. The divorce was being finalized. The kids would live with her. I wanted to reach out to something—to God, or just something that could hold me up a little while longer. Yet all I felt was trapped, trapped in a bruised and broken body, trapped in a hospital bed and tethered to a tangle of wires and tubes. Trapped by my regrets about the past.

On Christmas Eve I slept fitfully all evening. The pain only seemed to get worse. Sometime later that evening I snapped awake to shuffling feet and what I thought were chirping sounds. I blinked my eyes, not entirely convinced of what I was seeing. A gaggle of children traipsed noisily into my room. They were wrapped in scarves and mufflers. *What's this?* I wondered.

A woman brought up the rear. She cleared her throat, then signaled for them to sing. They began with some upbeat Christmas songs. Then, softly, the children intoned, "Silent night, holy night...." I raised my head. The rituals of my own childhood came drifting back to me on the familiar strains of music, so far off yet so close. Then they were done, shuffling out of my room and on to the next patient.

"Looks like Christmas is going to pass me by this year," I said to the woman.

"Don't ever talk like that," she whispered, as she left. "On Christmas, no one gets left behind."

I drifted off again, those words floating in my head. I was vaguely aware of a nurse checking my vital signs and of another adjusting my IV bag. Voices rose and fell outside in the hallway as visitors to other rooms came and went. Every so often a spasm of pain would bring me around, like someone stepping on an accelerator connected to my consciousness. I would shift and eventually the pain would subside a bit, but never completely.

MANUELLO PAGANELLI

**GREAT ADVENTURER** *Sal roams far and wide in search of ancient mysteries.*

Near midnight a nurse came to draw blood and fluff my pillow. When she left, the ICU was quiet, except for the distant chatter of a television. I'd never felt so alone in my life, desperately alone. Finally, almost irresistibly, a thought formed in my mind, more of a plea than a prayer. *God, am I really all alone?*

I dozed off—I don't know for how long—but all at once I popped awake. I thought I heard my door open. I peered through the dark. An elderly woman entered the room, someone I hadn't ever seen before.

"Are you a new doctor?" I asked.

"No," she replied. "I'm a volunteer."

"What do you do?"

"I help people," she said.

**A REAL-LIFE INDIANA JONES**
*Sal at a prehistoric site on the island of Menorca off the coast of Spain*

"Help people?" I said, skeptically. She wasn't dressed like a hospital aide. More like someone's mother. Her eyes were bright and intense. And yet she radiated calm.

"Every doctor who comes in here wants to poke me," I said. "What is it you want?"

"Joy," she said.

I would have laughed if I could. Joy was the last thing I could feel, something I hadn't felt in quite some time. I tried to read the name on her hospital badge, but it was blurry. "May I hold your hand?" she asked. Without waiting for my reply, she slipped her smaller hand around mine.

"What are you doing?" I asked.

"I'm praying for you," she said.

Instinctively, I wanted to pull my hand away. But I couldn't. I was too weak. Then, from somewhere deep inside I felt a tingle, like an electric charge coursing through my body. The feeling moved up along my spine and into my chest, then it exploded in my mind, infusing me with light and energy and a power that was at once alien and innate. I would not have been surprised to see myself aglow like the lights on the monitors. And I knew it meant the same thing: that I was alive and would survive. That never again would I feel alone. What I felt now was something very certain and very real: joy.

"Thank you, Lord," I heard myself say. The words reverberated through me like a kind of healing. I looked at the old woman. She was talking softly, soothingly.

I couldn't understand her words. But I knew she was praying.

I must have finally fallen back asleep. When I awoke, it was already Christmas morning. And the elderly woman was gone.

Bright and early a nurse came in to check my monitors and draw blood.

"Is there a church or some social group that visits patients on Christmas Eve night?" I asked.

"Not that I know of," she said.

"No one was here?" I asked.

"Visiting hours were over," she told me, somewhat distractedly.

I started to tell the nurse about the elderly woman. But she seemed preoccupied. "Did you hear what I said?" I asked.

She didn't answer my question. Instead, she headed for the nurses' station and rang for the attending physician.

A little while later the whole critical-care team congregated around my bed. What was up?

"Mr. Trento..." the attending physician began, his brow furrowing.

"Yes?" I asked, preparing for the worst.

"We're very surprised by your readings." He paused. "They're normal," he said. "Somehow your kidneys seem to be working again."

"But...how?" I asked.

"We don't know," the doctor said. Then he shook his head and ordered some more tests. "We just don't know."

But I knew what the tests would say—that I was well again, though I had a long road to recovery ahead of me.

What no test would ever show was another kind of healing, and another kind of road, one I travel still to this day.

I will remember that night in critical care forever. Christmas Eve. When no one is left behind. When all is joy.

COURTESY SAL TRENTO

A PREVIEW FROM

# Daily Guideposts 2012

*"For behold, I bring you good tidings of great joy, which shall be to all people."* —Luke 2:10

Taking down the Christmas tree is my least favorite holiday chore. It's always so exciting to buy one, bring it home, string it with lights and hang the ornaments we've collected over the years. But taking it down? The tree is dry and brittle, pine needles drop to the ground, the ornaments look weary and I'm sad. I wish the singing, the gathering with friends and family, the joy, could go on and on. Last year I took down the tree in record time, just to get it over with. I boxed up the ornaments and lights, dragged the dried husk outside to the recycling bin, vacuumed the rugs and floor clean of every pine needle I could find and then glanced at my watch. "Forty-five minutes," I declared.

"Well," Carol said, "you missed this." She picked a little drummer boy up off the rug and dangled it from its gold string.

"I've put away the boxes already," I said.

"I'll leave it on the piano." There it sat, urging me not to give up on Christmas entirely. Couldn't I still feel the glow without lights and tinsel? Maybe Christmas wasn't something to be rushed away from but carried with me like the boy with his drum. I don't remember who finally put the ornament away, but I could smell the piney scent of Christmas for weeks—and sense its joy—whenever I ran the vacuum cleaner.

*All the good things in life, Lord, were meant to be lingered over.*

—Rick Hamlin

DEBORAH ORY

*Daily Guideposts* is a book of uplifting devotionals. To order the 2012 edition, visit **guideposts.org/previewdgp** or write to Guideposts, P.O. Box 5815, Harlan, IA 51593-1315. The book is available in a hardcover version for $15.95 or in a softcover large-print version for $16.95, plus postage and processing.

# What Prayer

## Caring for *King*

NO CHILD should be left out at Christmas. That's why parties like the one for disabled children sponsored by a local lodge were so important. But I was anything but excited as I got dressed to go. *Please God,* I thought as I slipped on my dress shoes, *don't let King disrupt the party.*

My son, King, was five years old and autistic. He didn't like crowds. Or noise. Loud music sent him into a tantrum. Sometimes he lashed out at me or other children. I never knew what might set him off. My husband was working late, so I would have to handle any outbursts by myself. When we got to the party I was sure I'd made a mistake. So many people! So much noise! I longed to share the joy of Christmas with King, but would my prayers be enough to keep him calm?

I felt a tug on my hand. King pulled me into the room. He stared up at the Christmas tree and accepted a cookie and a toy from Santa. He watched the other children playing. If I didn't know better I'd say he was enjoying himself. *Don't kid yourself,* I thought. I stayed alert for the first sign of a meltdown. The band started a pounding rendition of "Jingle Bells." I got ready to carry King out. But instead of screaming, King bobbed his head. Families filled the floor, dancing together. King hopped up and down. He moved his feet to the beat. *He's dancing!* I thought. King took my hand. We swayed and spun together until we fell down laughing.

I'd thought such joy was beyond reach. What better time than Christmas for God to remind me that with him nothing is out of reach. Not for me, nor for King.

*Ann Richard*
*Pensacola, Florida*

## Strength in *Numbers*

Guideposts Classic 1997

DURING HER teens my daughter, Sandy, moved in with her father, whom I had divorced when she was little. Though I was hurt, I tried to remain upbeat. She didn't reach out to me, so I made all the calls and wrote all the letters. I was afraid that if I stopped, I would lose her. After she graduated from high school I knew I had to let go. By Christmas of 1991 we had not spoken in six months. Our relationship seemed hopeless. I had recently joined a new church. One Sunday I got up the courage to ask four women I respected to pray for Sandy and me every day for one year. They agreed to help. As the months passed, the support of those women filled

# Can Do

me with a peace I had never known before. Each morning I suspended my worries as I prayed, *Lord, help Sandy find the love that is waiting for her.*

On Christmas Eve, 1992, almost a year after my friends and I began praying, a card arrived from Sandy. The note inside read, "I am willing to try if you are." I was more than willing. Prayers aren't always answered overnight, but I know prayers are answered.

*Carol Ann McGiffin*
*Mount Airy, Maryland*

## Texas-Size *Miracle*

BRIGHT AND sunny—that was the typical weather forecast in Texas in December. So I was surprised when my 14-year-old daughter, Samantha, looked wistfully out the car window and wished for snow. "Just once I'd like to have a white Christmas," she said.

"Why don't we pray for it?"

"Really?" Samantha said. She bowed her head.

I said my own prayer as I drove. *God, I know this is Texas...but could you please send us a white Christmas?*

By the time I got home, reality had set in. *Snow? In Texas?* I totally understood if God didn't come through on this impossible request. But on Christmas Eve I noticed Samantha looking out the window more than usual. I just knew she was watching for snow. *Maybe she's not too old to believe the impossible,* I thought as we left for church.

At the end of the service we walked outside to pellets of white hail bouncing off the pavement. The air was saturated with icy moisture. It wasn't snow, but it was the closest thing we got here in southern Texas. "Wow!" Samantha said. *Thank you, God,* I thought. He'd let Samantha know he was listening, even if he didn't produce a Texas-size miracle.

Halfway home the hail turned to tiny flakes, which got larger and larger until we were driving through a genuine snowstorm. The first we'd ever seen in Corpus Christi!

At home Samantha jumped out of the car. She ran around, arms outstretched, and caught snowflakes on her tongue. I joined in, sliding on the freshly covered sidewalk.

Late that night I clicked on the weather station. Turns out, ours was the only area in Texas that got snow. Impossible? Without God in his heaven, yes.

*Evangelina Casarez*
*Corpus Christi, Texas*

**MAY WE PRAY FOR YOU?** Our volunteers meet on Monday mornings at 9:45. Write to Guideposts Prayer Fellowship, P.O. Box 5813, Harlan, IA 51593-1313, call (203) 778-8063 or visit our website at **OurPrayer.org** to post a prayer request or to join our online prayer community.

Merry Christmas!

PETER LAMASTRO

# The Joy of Holiday Cooking

*"Oh, bring us some figgy pudding..."*

—FROM "WE WISH YOU A MERRY CHRISTMAS"

# From *My Kitchen* to Yours

## When this celebrated writer puts down her pen, she picks up a spoon

**by Debbie Macomber, Port Orchard, Washington**

CHRISTMAS and cooking have always been linked for me. In my earliest memory I'm in the kitchen with my mother at Christmastime. Mom made beautiful plates of cookies and candies that she gave to family and friends. She spent days baking, stirring and rolling out dough, the room filled with tantalizing smells. On this day she must have asked me to help. What an honor. There I am, my small hands rolling warm chocolate into balls that Mom then dipped in more chocolate. Soon they would go onto one of the plates she assembled and decorated with big red bows. The best of Christmas is wrapped up in that memory: family, tradition, giving, food.

I'm a writer and a novelist and spend many hours in my office, but the kitchen is my favorite room in the house. Like my mother, I'm always cooking. I love trying out a new recipe. I rarely make the same thing twice, except for family favorites. A friend says that when we get together one of the first things I'll do is exclaim, "Have I told you about this new recipe I just found?" and then I'll jot it down. I adore cookbooks. I have shelves and shelves of them, ones I've collected over the years. But then, some of my best recipes are things that were passed along for generations before they were written down.

Take my mother's rice stuffing. Mom made it every Thanksgiving and Christmas, following a recipe she got from *her* mother. Sometimes if we were preparing dinner at my house she would arrive with the celery and onions and spices already browned in butter, so I never knew what the exact ingredients were. The first time I made the stuffing on my own after she died I couldn't get the seasonings right. I asked my husband, Wayne, and my children if something was missing and everybody said it was good, but I knew it wasn't exactly Mom's.

Naturally I looked through the cookbooks on my shelves. I tried one thing and another. I even consulted a family treasure, a simple brown notebook like the ones we used to use in school. On its yellowed pages my grandmother had written out all her favorite recipes for my mom. There's not an exact measurement in it, just a "pinch" of this, a "dash" of that, a "heaping portion"

KATE BALDWIN

of the other. She had immigrated to America from the Black Sea area of the Ukraine in the late nineteenth century and this was her legacy as a wife, mother and cook. But do you think there's a recipe for rice stuffing in my grandmother's neat handwriting? Not a chance.

What a mom cooks for her family can change over the years. When the children were little I slaved over a hot stove to make a big Christmas dinner like Mom used to do—turkey, rolls, stuffing, potatoes. Problem was, on Christmas day, the kids were more interested in their toys and Wayne was usually busy with a wrench assembling bikes and scooters. So instead I started to put together a Christmas buffet with everybody's favorite foods and we ate more leisurely. More recently, with our four kids all grown, we do the Macombers' Progressive Family Dinner. On the weekend before Christmas we go from house to house for a magnificent feast—first the soup at one place, then appetizers at another, then salads and finally the main course at ours with desserts. It takes all afternoon and we have a wonderful time.

Christmas wouldn't be Christmas without giving, and I think the best presents are those that come from hands and hearts, whether knit, crocheted, cooked or baked. For several years my daughters and

**ALWAYS COOKING**
*For Debbie, the kitchen is the heart of the home, especially at Christmastime.*

I got together for a slumber party to make Christmas treats to give away. We went through reams of recipes and no one got much sleep. I even wondered if we should put warning labels on some of the cookies: "Baked After Midnight with Much Joy and Laughter and Probably Not Enough Attention to the Directions!"

I know there are some cooks who keep their secret recipes under lock and key, but I've always been glad to share my favorites with anybody. After my first few novels were published I had collected the names and addresses of several hundred readers. At Christmas I wanted to do something for them as a thank-you. All I could think of was food. I printed a little cookbook of our family's best recipes, small enough to fit in a business-sized envelope, and mailed it off to over 300 people. A small present but a gift from the heart.

That tradition continues with the recipes I'd like to share with you here, selections from my newest book, *Debbie Macomber's Christmas Cookbook*. You'll see one of the desserts we prize, a main course and now, written down for the first time, my mother's delicious rice stuffing. Remember how I told you there was some ingredient missing? Not anymore. Just last year I was on a trip to Turkey, not far from the Black Sea, and as I was eating a rice salad I finally put my finger on it—the seasoning I had sought for years. I won't give it away. It's right there in the directions, a little taste of Christmas to pass along to you.

## Savory Herb-Roasted Chicken

- 6 tablespoons unsalted butter, at room temperature
- 2 tablespoons chopped fresh parsley, plus 6 large sprigs
- 2 tablespoons chopped fresh thyme, plus 6 large sprigs
- 2 tablespoons chopped fresh rosemary, plus 6 small sprigs
- Salt and black pepper
- 2 whole chickens (3½ to 4 pounds each), rinsed and patted dry
- 1 lemon, quartered
- 8 garlic cloves, smashed

Combine butter, chopped herbs and about ½ teaspoon salt; stir until blended. Preheat oven to 375°F; set rack in bottom third of oven. Season inside cavity of chickens with salt and pepper; stuff with lemon pieces, garlic and herb sprigs. Starting at neck end, slide fingers under skin of breast and upper part of legs, loosening skin. For each bird, scoop up 2 tablespoons of the herb butter and spread under skin. Place chickens breast-side up on racks in roasting pan; tie legs together loosely. Spread top and sides with remaining herb butter; sprinkle with salt and pepper.

Roast about 1½ hours, occasionally basting with pan juices. Chicken is done when thermometer inserted in thickest part of thigh registers 165°F. Transfer chickens to a board; let rest 10 minutes before carving. Serves 8. **Tip:** Chicken can be prepped and stuffed up to a day ahead. Cover and refrigerate. Bring to room temperature before continuing recipe.

# Mom's Rice Stuffing with Water Chestnuts, Apples & Hazelnuts

- 6 tablespoons unsalted butter
- 1 large onion, finely chopped
- 2 celery stalks, thinly sliced
- 2 tablespoons fresh thyme, chopped (That's it!)
- 2½ cups white rice
- 5 cups reduced-sodium chicken broth
- 1 8-ounce can water chestnuts, drained and chopped
- 2 tart apples, peeled and chopped
- 1½ cups hazelnuts, toasted, peeled and coarsely chopped
- 4 scallions, thinly sliced
- 1 cup raisins
- ½ cup chopped fresh parsley

Salt and black pepper

Melt butter in heavy large pot over medium heat. Add onion, celery and thyme; cook 6 minutes, stirring often. Add rice and broth; bring to a simmer. Reduce heat to low; cover and cook 22 minutes without stirring, until liquid is absorbed and rice is tender. Stir in water chestnuts, apples, hazelnuts, scallions, raisins and parsley. Season with salt and pepper.

If stuffing turkey: Loosely fill cavity with dressing. Place any leftover dressing in a buttered casserole dish. Cover with buttered foil, buttered-side down. Bake dressing for 30 minutes at 350°F, or until heated through.

If not stuffing turkey: Preheat oven to 350°F. Butter a 15x10-inch glass or ceramic baking dish. Stir ½ cup turkey drippings into dressing; spoon into dish. Cover with buttered foil, buttered-side down. Bake for 40 minutes, or until heated through. Serves 12 to 16.

# Red Velvet Cake

**Cake**

- 2½ cups cake flour
- ¼ cup unsweetened cocoa
- 1½ teaspoons baking powder
- 12 tablespoons unsalted butter, at room temperature, plus more for pans
- 2 cups granulated sugar
- 3 large eggs
- 1 teaspoon vanilla extract
- ¼ teaspoon salt
- 2 1-ounce bottles liquid red food coloring
- 3 tablespoons brewed coffee
- 1 cup buttermilk
- 1 tablespoon white vinegar
- 1 teaspoon baking soda

**Frosting**

- 1 8-ounce box cream cheese, at room temperature
- 8 tablespoons unsalted butter, at room temperature
- 1 teaspoon vanilla extract
- 4 cups sifted confectioner's sugar

Preheat oven to 350°F. Lightly butter three 6-inch pans for a small, tall cake, or two 9-inch pans for a traditionally sized cake. Line with parchment paper; butter and flour pans. In medium bowl, sift together flour, cocoa and baking powder. In large bowl mix butter and sugar on high speed until light and fluffy. Add eggs, beating well after each. Add vanilla, salt, food coloring and coffee; beat until combined. Reduce speed to low; alternately add dry ingredients and buttermilk. Beat until just combined.

In a small bowl, combine vinegar and baking soda. Add to batter; beat until blended. Pour batter into pans. Bake until toothpick inserted in center comes out clean, 25 minutes for small pans, 30 for larger pans. Cool on rack for 15 minutes, then turn cakes out and cool completely.

For frosting: In large bowl mix cream cheese and butter on high speed until fluffy. Beat in vanilla. Gradually add confectioner's sugar, beating until fluffy. Frost cake as desired; put in refrigerator to set.

# Pass It On

Some of our favorite holiday memories from your holiday tables

## Christmas Coupons

NOTHING BEAT my neighbor Candy's pies for dessert, so I was thrilled when she arrived at my house for Christmas Eve supper with one in her hand.

"For you," Candy said. "And a little something else too."

Candy gave me a green envelope tied with red ribbon. *Probably a nice Christmas card,* I thought. But inside were 12 index cards. Each one bore the same message: "This coupon entitles you to a pie whenever you need it!"

I thanked Candy that Christmas Eve, but it wasn't until the New Year rolled around that I really appreciated her amazing gift. On Valentine's Day my husband and I shared a romantic cherry pie for two. When my son made the basketball team we celebrated with Candy's heavenly silk chocolate. And come October, when weeks of dreary rain brought my spirits low, I cashed in a coupon for my favorite lemon meringue.

Christmas comes but once a year. But thanks to Candy, every month in between was sweet!

*—Hope B. Friedmann*

## Ohio Christmas Breakfast

BACK IN Ohio where I grew up, Christmas morning always meant a feast for breakfast. My mother made grit, a vanilla pudding, to go along with our bacon and French toast. But before we dug in, there were other mouths to be fed.

"Ready?" my father said after I'd pulled on my long underwear and boots.

"Ready."

We tromped outside, our arms full of carrots, suet, celery and straw. These we piled into the back of our station wagon. I climbed in beside Daddy and off we went to the nearest open field.

"There's a good spot!" I said, pointing to a little clump of trees.

PETER LAMASTRO

Guideposts Classic 1981

We carried our shovels over and cleared the snow away. Then we laid the food out on the ground. "Merry Christmas!" I called out to the trees.

Daddy took my hand and we marched back to the car. As I got in I looked back at the little clump of trees. A couple of squirrels were already checking out the feast with some crows. Soon they were joined by rabbits, opossums and deer.

When we got back to the house the aroma of bacon and cinnamon filled the air. Christmas breakfast was all the more delicious with the knowledge that our wild neighbors were enjoying it too.

—*Judy Rogers*

## A Christmas Autograph

YOU CAN NEVER have too many friends for Christmas dinner. That was the motto in our house. Unfortunately, with so many at the table year after year, sometimes it was hard to remember exactly everyone who'd shared our holiday meal.

Then my mother came up with a solution. "Why don't we have all the guests leave their signature?" she said.

"You mean like in a guest book?" I asked.

Mom shook her head. "Not exactly," she said. "I was thinking they could sign the tablecloth."

The idea sounded crazy enough that it just might work. Before we laid out the dishes Christmas Eve we passed out thick black pens. The guests loved it. But I wondered, *What's going to happen when we wash the tablecloth?* Those Christmas dinners left a lot of spills.

Mom took charge of the cloth after the holiday. A few weeks later she unfurled it for me. The signatures had been embroidered over, along with the date. Now they would never come out in the wash!

Over the years our Christmas tablecloth got pretty crowded with names. The more full it got, the more I cherished it. You can never have too many friends for Christmas dinner.

—*Isabelle Calvachio*

## CHRISTMAS DILEMMA:
## You spend too much time in the kitchen

## SOLUTION:
# Soup's On!

**by Anne Riess, Unity, Saskatchewan, Canada**

I TOOK A PEEK at the grocery carts ahead of me in the checkout line. Turkey, turkey and more turkey. "We sell so many birds this time of year it's amazing we can keep them stocked," the cashier said to no one in particular.

"My family looks forward to turkey dinner all year," the woman behind me said.

I had no turkey. My cart was filled with onions. Were we really going to skip turkey dinner on Christmas? The idea to make French onion soup instead came from my kids. They'd loved the rich scent of it simmering on the stove one chilly afternoon. "It smells just like Christmas!" they claimed. Soup wasn't very traditional. But it was simple and easy to make. *Maybe I'd actually enjoy Christmas morning if I wasn't slaving away over a turkey,* I thought.

"I can make a turkey anytime," I'd explained to my husband. "I want to make Christmas memories with you and the kids, not be stuck in the kitchen basting a bird."

I guess you could say I talked him into it. But now that I was shopping for our Christmas dinner, I felt self-conscious. The cashier looked at me funny when she rang up my onions. I paid without explaining.

Christmas Eve found me without any food prep chores. I played board games with the kids, snuggled with my husband on the couch and the whole family went ice-skating. Before bed we read the Christmas story from the Bible. My last thought was whether I should run out to find a premade turkey with all the fixings.

After a glorious Christmas morning with very little time spent in the kitchen, we sat down at a candlelit table laid with our best dishes. I made sure the bread was warm and crunchy, with soft butter on the side. I ladled out the soup. It was a lot easier than the turkey-cutting ritual we'd had in years past. Maybe too easy. Could Christmas dinner be special without it?

"I'd like to say a blessing," my husband said. "Thank you, God, for this Christmas and all the Christmases we've had around this table."

"Amen," the kids said. *Yes,* I thought. *That's what we should be thankful for.* Not turkey basted for hours or cranberry sauce, no matter how sweet. But fully enjoying one another's presence. I couldn't think of a better tradition than that.

## French Onion Soup

- 3 pounds onions, diced
- 1½ tablespoons butter
- 3 cups beef broth
- 3 cups chicken broth
- 1 tablespoon instant coffee
- Pepper (to taste)
- Croutons
- Sliced mozzarella cheese

Sauté onions in butter and transfer to a large soup pot. Simmer broth, onions, coffee and pepper together for several hours (at least three). Then pour soup into individual ovenproof bowls. Top each bowl with croutons and mozzarella cheese. Bake at 350°F for 20 to 25 minutes. Serve with a warm loaf of hearty bread. Serves 6 to 8.

PHOTOS BY REBECCA SAHN

CHRISTMAS DILEMMA:
## You live in a new town and miss your old friends

SOLUTION:
# Ladies' Brunch!

**by Jenny Landes, Edmond, Oklahoma**

SPRIGS OF evergreen rested among lighted garlands on our fireplace mantel. I wove a ribbon between the boughs. *Too bad there's no one to enjoy it besides us,* I thought. Back home in El Dorado, Arkansas, our house was always full of friends, family and neighbors at Christmas. But when my husband, Rodney, landed a job in Oklahoma City, we'd had to move. It was months later and it still didn't feel like home to me.

In El Dorado we'd had so many activities at Christmastime, I had to chart them on a calendar to keep track. Entertaining was how we connected with friends.

I took a break from my decorating and went to the mailbox, but there were only catalogs inside. *God, couldn't you find me some friends to celebrate with this Christmas?* Then I got an idea: What if I threw a party myself?

"A ladies' holiday brunch," I told Rodney. "I'm hosting it."

"You used to love to do that sort of thing," he said.

"You're right!"

I had e-mail addresses from the kids' school. I chose a Christmassy border for my invitation, typed in the specifics and hit *Send.* The minute I did I got nervous. *What if no one responds?* After all, I wasn't in Arkansas anymore. *Have a little faith,* I told myself.

My worrying was interrupted by a *ding* from my inbox. My first "yes"! Throughout the day more RSVPs came in. I flipped through recipes to put together the perfect menu. It felt like Christmas already.

The night before the party, I stayed up late making egg casserole and stuffing almonds into dates. Rodney pitched in, mixing up sausage balls. These were all crowd-pleasers back home in Arkansas. The timer buzzed and I took a loaf of cranberry bread from the oven. I waited till the next morning to heat up some spiced tea, and then popped the bacon-wrapped dates into the oven after some cinnamon rolls. One hour to go. I brewed coffee and arranged serving platters on the dining table.

The doorbell rang. "Your house looks beautiful," my first guest said. She helped herself to the party foods while I welcomed someone else. Soon carols from the radio mingled with the laughter of two dozen women. The house brimmed with Christmas spirit!

As I set out another plate of bacon-wrapped dates, a mother from my daughter's class leaned in. "Thanks for hosting this party, Jenny. Your friends seem so nice."

*My friends?* I thought. *Yes, my friends.* It would take time to make the kind of friendships I'd cultivated for over a decade back home, but I was off to a good start now. All I needed was a little faith, delicious food and some old-fashioned Arkansas-style hospitality.

## Stuffed Dates

- 1 8-oz. bag whole pitted dates
- 40 whole almonds
- 10 bacon slices, cut in fourths

Stuff an almond into each date. Wrap dates with bacon and secure with a toothpick. Broil in oven until bacon is crispy, about 12 minutes. Makes about 40.

# Chocolate Chip Christmas

## She was a close friend—but ask her to share her trademark recipe? No way!

**by Arlene Hopkins, Scranton, Pennsylvania**

EARLY WINTER mornings in Pennsylvania are freezing cold, but that didn't keep me from my morning walk. I pulled on my gloves and stepped outside, breathing in the fresh air. I could already see the lights on at my friend Mary Ellen's house. That meant she was up and ready to walk with me. "How are your Christmas preparations coming?" I asked when she joined me outside.

"It seems like I'll never get everything done," she said. "Just like last year."

I couldn't imagine Mary Ellen having any trouble with the holidays. She was the best hostess in Green Ridge, the neighborhood where we lived. Every year I marveled at the way she decorated her home for her Christmas parties. Even more I marveled at the food she made. Martha Stewart had nothing on Mary Ellen.

"Are you making your chocolate chip cookies this year?" I asked as we walked down the tree-lined street toward St. Clare's church.

"Of course," she laughed. "It wouldn't be Christmas without those."

Of all Mary Ellen's famous dishes, her cookies were my favorite. I had a long, somewhat troubled, history with chocolate chip cookies. My Italian mother was a wonderful cook. She taught me the secret of the pasta and sauces that were her specialty. Fancy Italian pastries came out of our oven like magic, but she never got the hang of chocolate chip cookies. Those simple Toll House-style cookies, the kind I learned to love at my friends' houses, were a mystery to her.

As a teenager I'd spent hours trying—and failing—to master them. One batch was burned around the edges. Another was rock hard. "I'll never get them right!" I said one night after pulling yet another tray of bland cookies out of the oven.

"Your cookies are the best I've ever tasted," I told Mary Ellen, trying to hide the envy in my voice. "I don't know how you do it."

"Secret recipe," she said. "I learned it as a young girl. If you follow the instructions to the letter you can't go wrong."

BAKING BUDDIES
*Arlene (left) has joined Mary Ellen (right) as a chocolate chip cookie master.*

PHOTOS BY PAUL PUGLIESE

*I wonder if she'd give that recipe to me,* I thought. In all the time Mary Ellen and I had been walking buddies we'd talked about cooking—and those cookies—many times, but I'd never asked for the recipe. How could I? Now the conversation turned to other things. *At least I'll get to enjoy the cookies at Mary Ellen's Christmas party,* I reminded myself.

But when I stepped into my kitchen a few days later to work on my own Christmas dishes, those cookies were all I could think about. "Mary Ellen says the recipe is foolproof," I told my husband. "Maybe even I couldn't mess it up. I know how much you love chocolate chip cookies."

"It can't hurt to ask her," said Dave. "The worst that could happen is she would say no."

*But what if I upset her by asking?* I thought the next morning as I got ready for our walk. Little things like that can cause trouble between friends. I returned to my house again without the recipe. *Besides,* I thought, *I could never make anything as well as Mary Ellen does.*

I put the cookies out of my mind until a few days later, when Mary Ellen and I got talking about Christmas baking again. "I'm going to make twice as many cookies this year," she said. "I always run out."

"Do you think you could ever give me the recipe?" I said.

For a moment Mary Ellen didn't say a word. *Uh-oh,* I thought. *I just lost my walking buddy.* "I'm sorry!" I said quickly. "It's your special recipe. You shouldn't share it with me. That wouldn't be fair."

A smile quirked Mary Ellen's mouth. "You may be right," she said. "That wouldn't be fair. Unless..."

I leaned forward eagerly.

"Unless you gave me the recipe for that marinara sauce of yours!" Mary Ellen said. "I've tried and tried with my own sauce and I just can't do it like you!"

My chocolate chip cookies are no longer burned, rock hard or bland. There's a trick to getting them right—several tricks, all of which are laid out in Mary Ellen's recipe. Everyone who tries them says they're the best they've ever tasted. I tell them I owe it all to my friend Mary Ellen, the best chocolate chip cookie baker in town.

I hear her marinara sauce isn't too bad either.

**SECRET NO MORE**
*There are several tricks to making the perfect cookie.*

## "Tricky" Chocolate Chip Cookies

- 1 stick margarine, softened (Imperial works well)
- 1 egg
- 1 cup white sugar
- ½ cup oil
- ½ cup packed dark brown sugar
- 1 teaspoon baking soda
- 1 teaspoon salt
- 1 teaspoon vanilla
- 2¼ cups flour
- 6 to 8 ounces semisweet chocolate chips

Combine margarine, egg, sugar, oil and brown sugar (in that order*) with electric mixer. By hand, mix in baking soda, salt, vanilla and flour. Then add chocolate chips. Refrigerate dough for 1 hour.* Preheat oven to 375°F. Spray cookie sheets with cooking spray. Drop dough by rounded teaspoon, 12 per tray. Bake for 10 minutes on the top rack only* (bake one tray at a time*). Check cookies at 9 minutes to be sure not to overcook them. *Cool on wire rack. Makes about 48.

*Trick!

# Abundant Table

*Thank you, Lord, for all you've given us; for this feast, for our gifts, for our health and especially for the love we share on this, your holy birthday.*

BARBARA FEAD, CINCINNATI, OHIO

## Easy, Healthy Homemade Granola

- 2 cups rolled oats
- 1 teaspoon cinnamon
- 1 teaspoon salt
- 3 tablespoons plus 1 teaspoon vegetable oil
- ¼ cup honey
- ¼ cup light brown sugar, firmly packed
- 1 teaspoon pure vanilla extract
- ⅓ cup whole almonds
- ⅓ cup whole hazelnuts
- ⅓ cup golden raisins
- ⅓ cup dried cherries

Preheat oven to 325°F. Line a baking sheet with parchment paper. In large bowl, toss oats with cinnamon and salt. In medium bowl, stir together oil, honey, brown sugar and vanilla. Whisk till combined. Pour honey mixture over oats; use hands to combine. Pour onto prepared baking sheet. Spread out evenly, but leave a few clumps for texture. Bake for 10 minutes. Remove from oven and use a spatula to flip granola. Sprinkle almonds over granola; return baking sheet to oven. Bake 5 minutes. Remove from oven and flip granola. Sprinkle hazelnuts over granola and return baking sheet to oven for 10 minutes. Remove from oven and let cool. Sprinkle raisins and cherries over granola, then transfer to an airtight container. Makes 1 pound.